life begins

Copyright © 2018 Norwich Youth for Christ

All rights reserved. This book or any portion thereof may not be reproduced or used in any manner whatsoever without the express written permission of the publisher except for the use of brief quotations in a book review or scholarly journal.

First Printing: 2018

ISBN 978-0-9956107-6-7

Norwich Youth for Christ,

36 St Giles Street

Norwich, NR2 1LL
www.norwichyfc.co.uk

Printed by CZ Design & Print 01279 657769

Disclaimer: While every attention has gone into detail, this book is a collection of memories and stories and as such we recognise that some dates, names and information may not be completely accurate.

Scriptures taken from the Holy Bible, New International Version®, NIV®. Copyright © 1973, 1978, 1984, 2011 by Biblica, Inc.™ Used by permission of Zondervan. All rights reserved worldwide. www.zondervan.com The "NIV" and "New International Version" are trademarks registered in the United States Patent and Trademark Office by Biblica, Inc.™

Index

Introduction 1

Glossary 4

Foreword by Neil O'Boyle 6

Andy Clarke 8

Ang Fox 10

Ann Rudland 12

Anna Linton 14

Azarias Harding 16

Becca Savory 18

Becky Kemp 20

Becs Wright 22

Ben Lawrence 23

Beth Goymer 25

Beth & Josh Mathieson 27

Chris Starling 29

Clive Calver 31

Daisy Palmer 33

Danny Ellero 34

Dave Gallop 36

David & Ann Adeney 38

Dave & Linda Howes	40
David Sims	41
Edward de Kam	43
Ellie Hawke	45
Ellie Rodd	47
Emma Craig	48
Eric Bone	50
Fliss Jones	54
Gavin Calver	57
Geoff Lawton	58
Graham James	60
Hazel Erskine	62
Heather Land	65
Helen Roberts	67
Ian Savory	69
John Dade	73
John Loaker	75
John McGinley	78
Johny Grimwood	80
Jonathan Richardson	82
Josie from Brazil	84
Joy Clark	86

Karen Coleman	91
Katie Clough	93
Katrina Harper	96
Keith Willers	98
Lauren Ellero	100
Margaret Smith	103
Mark Tuma	105
Martin Forster	108
Naomi Tate	110
Naomi Tuma	112
Neville Willerton	115
Nick Blanch	118
Paul Gowing	120
Pete Skivington	121
Phil Timson	123
Rachel Varley	125
Rob Wilson	127
Roy Crowne	129
Ruth MacCormack	131
Sally McNeish	132
Sarah Weller	134
Simon Faulks	135

Simon Kirby 137

Simon Oliver 139

Sophie Gathercole 141

Steph Richardson 144

Steve Biltawi 147

Stuart Riddington 150

Susanna Bornman 152

Thea Smith 154

Tim Yau 157

Tracey Hyslop 159

Wioletta Williams 162

Afterword 164

Introduction

This book is another one of those crazy ideas that often surfaces in the minds and discussions of people who work at Norwich Youth for Christ. At first it seems ridiculous - we could never publish a book! Then you start digging and doing some research and it seems even more ridiculous! But then a plan starts to come together, you start to step out and then God provides the resources to make it happen. This has been a yearlong project for me and I'm so glad to have got to the finish line (that doesn't happen so neatly with young people!).

In this book you will find over seventy stories from young people, staff, volunteers, some who fit all of those categories and even opportunities where Norwich Youth for Christ has been a catalyst for other YFC centres in the UK and beyond!

As impressive as this sounds, I honestly believe this only scratches the surface of what God has done through the organisation over the last four decades. I know there are so many more stories that are untold, some just because we had deadlines to meet but others because we have simply lost touch or don't know the impact of the seeds that were sown. As much as this is a testimony to what God is doing in us, I hope it serves as an encouragement to what God is doing through your church, youth work or ministry. When you are in the midst of it, so often it feels like two steps forwards and three steps back and we wonder if we are making progress. As you read these stories, recognise that is how those involved probably felt at the time as well. We rarely get to see the bigger picture of what

God is doing so remember that nothing is wasted, God is at work and He is doing immeasurably more than you could ever ask or imagine. Remember this truth for your family, your neighbours, your ministry, your church.

'Therefore, my dear brothers and sisters, stand firm. Let nothing move you. Always give yourselves fully to the work of the Lord, because you know that your labour in the Lord is not in vain.'
1 Corinthians 15:58

Not heard of Youth for Christ? I'm not sure how this book found its way to you but let me tell you about this amazing movement of Jesus followers. We're about seeing young people's lives changed by Jesus. We do this by showing Jesus in a way that is relevant to every young person. Through our varied projects and clubs, we demonstrate the love of God, declare who Jesus is, offer opportunities to decide to follow Him and disciple young people to live their lives to the full. There are over seventy local YFC centres across the UK and Norwich Youth for Christ is one of them. We are a family together and yet each YFC centre is distinct as its own charity, locally focused and with locally driven projects delivered in collaboration with the churches in the area. This means our support comes locally as well. Just by buying this book you have helped support our work. Thank you! But I wonder if I could ask you to consider being a stronger part of who we are. As you read through these pages, ask yourself if you could give a little each month to help continue this incredible work and maybe, in another 40 years, someone will publish a sequel.

I'd like to say a few thanks to some special people that enabled this book to be written. Thanks to my amazing wife Becca who planted the thought of a book in my head and helped to proofread. I really must listen to her more! Thanks to everyone who contributed a story, even when I was harassing you to meet the deadlines. This book would not have happened without you! I have loved reading your stories and each one is precious and an encouragement to the current team. Thanks to all those who wanted to contribute but who couldn't meet the deadline! I am truly grateful for everyone who even expressed a willingness to help as it helped us to persevere and keep going with it. Thanks to my incredible Office Managers, Fliss Jones and Becca Savory, for getting quotes, contacting people, sorting through photos and so many other fiddly things that I didn't have the time to do! Thank you to our trustees who agreed to take a risk and use some of our budget to publish this. The proceeds of this book will go back into our budget and so hopefully it will generate some funds - but there is no guarantee of that! Again, it's another example of the faith of our trustees and they are a real blessing. Thanks to David Adams and Margaret Smith for proofreading at the last minute! Thanks to Ben Lawrence who put the design together with tight timescales and the busyness of everything else that is going on. Thanks to the staff team, who have been incredibly supportive and patient when my time was focused on this project. Finally, thanks be to God who graciously answers our prayers and invites us to join in the adventure of a life lived with Jesus! It's not easy, but it is worthwhile.

Nick Blanch
Director, 2018
Norwich Youth for Christ

Glossary

We've tried to ensure every story makes sense, but as there have been so many projects with distinctive names, we thought it may help to have a list of them in one handy place!

BYFC – British Youth for Christ

Detached – Youth work that happens on the street, or in a space with no resources or building attached.

Encounter – A youth worship service

Express – A themed, fast paced, youth event for 11 – 14's

The Forum – A social media project where young people could join our moderated discussion board discussing life, building community and asking faith questions.

Fridays - A youth worship service held on a ...Friday!

Ikon / Ritzy's - A nightclub in Norwich which we worked at regularly with our nightclub ministry

The Jam – A weekly music club for young people aimed at developing music and media skills

Living Water - Christian camp/conference held at The Royal Norfolk Showground over May weekend. At its peak it was attended by over 3000 people.

NYFC – Norwich Youth for Christ

Newday – A Christian summer camp /conference for young people held at the Royal Norfolk Showground.

Op Gid / Operation Gideon - a gap year scheme. Those on the scheme were known as Op Gids.

SOGITS – Serious on God Intensive Training - A discipleship group for emerging young leaders

Soul Survivor – A Christian summer camp / conference for young people held at the Royal Bath and West Showground.

Supanova - A project run in Ikon which was an under 16's nightclub.

'Who Cares?' – A county wide mission asking the question 'What hurts the most?' to general public to understand some of the biggest issues in our area. We did a youth version and asked the same question to as many young people as possible in schools and youth clubs, to help give us an idea on how we could deal with some of the biggest issues facing young people.

Foreword

At Youth for Christ, we are about seeing young people's lives changed by Jesus, for 40 years Norwich Youth for Christ has faithfully taken good news relevantly across the city and surrounding areas. Countless young people whether it be through clubs, camps, schools, detached work or church events have heard the Gospel by passionate youth for Christ staff and volunteers over the years. What a legacy! What a history! What a difference!

I remember as I pioneered a local Youth for Christ Centre over 20 years ago looking on with great admiration at Norwich, viewed by many to be a flag ship ministry. Ian Savoury was the Centre Director and I would watch with interest at the way in which he led his team, listened to the reports on the many opportunities that they had by given, and heard the stories of transformed lives. I could not help but conclude there was a real sense of favour on this particular ministry. Now years later, again I watch on with great respect for the ministry led by Nick Blanch as he continually explores with the team new opportunities to relevantly take good news. The ministry has at no point remained idle, rather pushed the boundaries, and led the way. Norwich Youth for Christ remains a model example to the British Youth for Christ family of how youth ministry can effectively be done.

The old faithful motto of Youth for Christ International is 'anchored to the rock, geared to the times.' May Norwich always remain relevant to young people while rooted in the truths of the Bible. As the founder of our worldwide movement, Torrey Johnson, said towards the end of his life reflecting on the ministry of Youth for Christ "The past was great, the present is better, but the best is yet to come." May the best years of Norwich Youth for

Christ remain ahead of them. However, may we remain exceptionally grateful for its faithfulness to both young people and the Gospel over the last 40 years!

Neil O'Boyle
National Director
Youth for Christ

Andy Clarke

On a crisp, clear Tuesday morning in November 1982, this young man woke up bright and early to set up his guitar and a ton of other equipment in the main hall of Thorpe Grammar School ready for assembly. It was his very first visit to Norwich and at the age of 19 also turned out to be one of the most significant moments at a very formative time of life. This was the day I met my wife. The occasion was provided by Norwich Youth for Christ who had invited national touring band The Reps to perform at several local schools throughout the week. Our volunteer roadie for the day was a student nurse called Joy whose parents John and Pearl Breeze from Oak Grove Chapel were putting up a couple of band members for the week. Joy was an ex-pupil of Thorpe Grammar who was then in her first year of training in London but happened to be home in Norwich at the time. She really could not believe that a rock band were going to play in her normally very formal school assembly and had to see this for herself! The band went down well not only that day in Thorpe Grammar but over the whole week of lessons, assemblies and lunchtime concerts which culminated in a packed-out concert at Chapelfield Methodist Church where many youngsters responded to the Gospel Message.

This story was the beginning of an amazing life journey for Joy and myself who, as a married couple, continued to tour as Double Check with many subsequent visits to schools in Norwich as a result of our relationship with NYFC initiated by Geoff Lawton and Grantley Watkins. Especially memorable was our work alongside the Bus Project with Danny Pritchard, Steve Bedford and Dave Townsend which enabled us to visit schools throughout Norfolk and see many young lives impacted by the message of

God's love for them. As part of our continuing relationship through Ian Savory at NYFC and then Oak Grove Chapel, we also had the opportunity to serve in the youth programme at Living Water for several years alongside Tracy Hyslop and more recently at YFC Spring Camp with Ang Fox and Ali Roberts.

Joy and I currently run national Youth for Christ touring band 'The Sense' along with their street dance crew 'Stance' and even now have ongoing opportunity to serve Nick and the NYFC team, most recently at their Encounter event. We were there earlier this year and as we drove up to unload the equipment we recognised that the venue, Norwich Central Baptist Church, was formerly St. Mary's where Joy and I were married some 33 years ago as result of our meeting on that bright November morning, all because of NYFC! So, we have much for which we thank Norwich Youth for Christ and the amazing people that have served there over the years, inspiring us by example of lives dedicated to reaching young people with the Good News of Jesus. We serve God wholeheartedly today because of you and we celebrate with you all that God has done, is doing, and will do in the years to come!

Andy Clarke
The Sense and *Stance* Coordinator
Youth for Christ

Ang Fox

What can I say about NYFC except ever since I was a baby Christian it has been a massive part of my Christian walk. I did not come to faith as a teenager but in my twenties. I first encountered NYFC at Hellesdon High School when Graham Kendrick came to teach us how to 'Make Way'. Ian Savory was just arriving and I remember a wheelbarrow being involved somehow and the toilets were blocked in the school. It was only a short time after that when I stood outside 14c Middletons lane that God clearly told me I would work for YFC. So there it began.

I danced in Thorpe High School as part of the worship band led by Bob Lloyd and met Mike Rice Pudding for the first time. I had a scary experience of teaching 150 young people a dance in a sports hall. As I became involved in Rock Solid I helped churches set up and run groups and went to a training session in Coventry with Tim Yau, who slept through most of the seminars…it made me realise how hard youth workers work! He had been busy working in a nightclub.

Whilst looking after Rock Solid, one of my most interesting visits to a club was in Acle where the leader had not considered the effect of flour and water together. After a lot of fun with the young people it took longer to clean the room than it did to deliver the youth work with paste everywhere.

I loved being part of an amazing team doing an exciting range of events such as Express at St Catherine's where the equipment was lowered through the roof much like the bed for the paralysed man.

The event took 10 hours to set up, 2 hours of meeting and 3 hours to dismantle. At one Express we had so many young people respond to the gospel we could not cater for them. Totally mad but lots of fun.

Finally being part of Spring Camp/Weekend working with Joy and Andy Clark who have such a heart for young people. This event has impacted so many young people over the years, many who are now leaders themselves. It is still running but no longer camping!

For me NYFC is about family and fun, relationship with God and reaching the youngsters, all for Christ.

Ang Fox

Ann Rudland

I have many happy memories of serving NYFC on the Executive Committee - Committee meetings were anything but dull with much hilarity surrounding getting the serious business of the evening done.

During my time with NYFC we were involved in many exciting projects but my outstanding memory was our involvement in December 1989 in the nationwide project "Christmas Cracker" (which in Norwich was organized by NYFC). The brainchild of Steve Chalke, the idea was that customers "eat less and pay more" for their meal, with simple meals being served at high street prices, in order to help raise money for charities working in India to alleviate the appalling poverty there.

Many months of preparation went on beforehand - seeking the support and sponsorship of local businesses, asking for the loan of equipment and above all securing some premises which proved very hard to find but after months of searching God provided a venue that turned out to be the largest in the country!!

Norwich property developer and keen Christian Graham Dacre had just bought the latterly rundown Bell Hotel right in the city centre and was happy for us to use it before he developed it in the New Year. Weeks of cleaning and painting followed (The inches of grease on its kitchen walls and surfaces weren't for the faint-hearted!!) with the young people giving up their October half-term to get everything ready in time. The project captured the imagination of local people and negotiations with various Council, and Health & Safety officials were made easier by the purpose of the restaurant and the commitment of the young people to it. And very unusually for the local press, they ran several articles about the venture even before the restaurant opened!

We'd had the practice runs and training sessions and now the Big Day had arrived! With several of the young people disguised as a giant Christmas Cracker, and the local press and tv in attendance, the Town Crier in full regalia heralded the Grand Opening before Anglia Television's cookery star, Patrick Anthony cut the ribbon to officially open the restaurant! Fantastic but then we realised that the Opening had been so successful in getting the attention of passers-by that around **eighty** people were coming into the restaurant to be served **all at once**!! Actually they were all very understanding and happy to wait. Just as well they couldn't see the mild panic going on behind the scenes!!

The popularity of the restaurant continued and we were all very encouraged that in just three weeks £18,000 was raised to help the poor in India. The young people were brilliant in their various roles which many customers commented on and there was a really happy atmosphere present throughout the whole time the restaurant was open.

Ann Rudland

Anna Linton

National Youth for Christ had accepted my gap year application. I packed my gigantic suitcase for the year and left Scotland with the biggest sense of adventure! I was not told where I was going to be placed until after I arrived for ten days of training in Lichfield. "Norwich? Where's that?" asked sixteen year old me, a young person myself. I didn't know a single thing about Norwich but I was certain of two things. The first - God had sent me. The second - I was so excited for what lay ahead.

Before heading to Norwich, I heard fantastic things about the centre and Nick Blanch, the centre Director. I was eager to meet this Nick Blanch, I'd heard so much about.

After my year I can confirm that what I'd heard was most definitely true! Norwich YFC is a strong centre and is gifted in bringing out the best in people. I was given opportunities as fast as I could take them. I felt particularly encouraged through prayer. The initial ten days of training is a very spirit led time with lots of worshiping, inspirational talks, Bible readings and lots of praying. I admitted to one of the girls that I couldn't pray out loud I just felt too self-conscious. Unhelpfully she told me how easy it was.

There were many points in the year were I was given the opportunity to pray. "Anna do you mind praying before we start?" "Anna do you want to pray with the young people for their week ahead?" "I'm new to church can you pray for me?" I really challenged myself to pray at every opportunity no matter how uncomfortable I felt. By the end of the year I was told I had the gift of intercession and a couple of people asked me if I'd take up praying for them. I never saw this gift in myself but it was recognized, discovered and developed by the staff at Youth for Christ.

This is one example of the many times Youth for Christ took time to encourage me, strengthen me, and help me grow in my faith. I was never afraid to try things and to fail. I have also witnessed this attitude with the young people. Norwich Youth for Christ will bend over backwards for the young people. Putting in extra time and resources to give young people opportunities they wouldn't otherwise get. The young people in Norwich are cared for individually on a deep level by the staff and my prayer for the centre is that it will continue to thrive and grow within the next forty years.

Anna Linton

Azarias Harding

Foundations aren't always that pretty or talked about that much but in the bible we learn how without the right foundations we could just wash away. That's what my gap year with Norwich Youth for Christ was, a foundational year. Though this foundational year was with some pretty amazing people and I will be talking about it for years to come.

Whenever you go and live somewhere, the real thing you miss after leaving are the people you left behind. Luckily, I don't live worlds apart from Norwich but it was the people that made my year so foundational. They all invested in me and wanted to see me thrive and grow in my relationship to my God and Heavenly Father. I remember once when I was in line management and I was told 'Azarias, you are so chatty but when it comes to group prayer, you are silent'. They challenged me to pray more openly when in a group. It was completely the right thing to challenge me on. I took that challenge and have been trying faithfully to be as open in prayer as I see God wants me to be. The year laid foundations for courage.

I have learnt that praying out loud in a group enriches your prayer life because we are all creations of communication and need to release that communication. It also helps those around you who are praying with you. They might have wondered off in thought, started thinking about what's for dinner, or just wouldn't of ever prayed for what you prayed for. Not because they are less holy but because each of us are unique and we might be praying for the same issue but seeing it from different perspectives. The year laid foundations for seeking unity.

While I was with Norwich YFC we produced many different videos, one was particularly personal as it was a testimony from myself about losing my earthly father and reaching out for my heavenly one. Since making that video, while I still miss my father, I have changed and my relationship with my heavenly has grown. I would probably say things differently now if I redid it and smile more but the truth that remains then, now and into my future. Is that I have a Father and I am a child of God. The year laid foundations for identity.

Being with Norwich YFC gave me the first real chance to live, see and work in a job where the team works so well because they rest together, have grace with one another, challenge each other and have fellowship. Who balances this? Well the one that stirs Norwich YFC - ultimately the Father, Son and Holy Spirit.

Azarias Harding

Becca Savory

My involvement with NYFC started with attending 'Fridays' when I was 15 years old. I now only have vague memories of this time but remember loving being with such a large number of Christian young people as the church I went to only had a few. I had been to Soul Survivor the year before with my church youth group and now I was able to regularly attend something closer to home that spiritually fed me in a similar way to the festival. At Fridays I had the opportunity to be part of the 'Blood of the Lamb' production, which took place in 1999. I really enjoyed being in this show, (I was a leper!) and making new friends. I remember sitting in the back of Ian Savory's car having a lift home from rehearsals – who knew 10 years later he would become my father-in-law!!

I continued to be part of Fridays and took part in the dedication service - the certificate I still have at home today. On one particular Fridays I was prayed for by Margie Bone and had a very real and peaceful experience of the Holy Spirit. Although I have had a relationship with God since a very young age, this was a significant event in my journey, as I felt my relationship with God became more personal from that day on.

For the next couple of years I took every opportunity I could to serve at Fridays and other NYFC events. I was part of the serving team at Fridays: helping to set up and pack down and run the OHP for worship eventually leading ice-breakers, leading talks and other upfront bits. I remember the first of these was interviewing Ross Paterson about his work in China. I was part of the team that ran Café Uno at New Wine in 2000, involved in F2 which launched in 2004, volunteered at SNAP dance at the then Ignite nightclub at

Riverside in 2004, was part of the team for Reality in 2006 and Reality II in 2007. I even have vague memories of working on the bus and volunteering at the NYFC charity shop. NYFC had a discipleship group for girls called SOGITS (still not sure what it stood for!) which I was part of.

Being a volunteer with NYFC during my mid to late teens has been such an important part of my life. I made some amazing friends, deepened my relationship with God, and as I served, I started to see some of the gifts I had and how I could use them.

In 2009 a job opportunity at NYFC arose – office manager maternity cover for Fliss Jones. I was working as a nurse at the time but this *temporary* change was something I felt drawn to. I ended up working at NYFC for 8 years and still volunteer today!!

NYFC has been part of my life for the last 19 years and I can honestly say I don't know where I would be now if it wasn't for those early days of Fridays. It has solidified my faith, taught me so much about who I am and whose I am, and I am very proud to say that 19 years later NYFC is still doing the same for young people today.

Becca Savory (née Forster)

Becky Kemp

Norwich YFC played such a deep part in my journey of getting to know Jesus during my late teens, and I will forever be thankful.

I found myself studying art in Norwich, having moved up from Luton, and was a bit of a wallflower, shall we say! Discovering that God was real, for me was a total game changer. It was the era of excitedly camping at Living Water, with a young Matt Redman leading worship, followed by the early years of a Jazz infused Phatfish, and of course Simon Oliver's untameable shenanigans on the youth site :) The presence of the Holy Spirit felt like home and I was experiencing the intimacy of God in such a heartfelt way.

I can definitely say that seeing NYFC staff and volunteers (both office based and those out on the field), leading and living it out (and sometimes prancing around in tutus) inspired me to want to go deeper. And one of the main vehicles of grasping this was at 'Fridays'. Realising that there was a community of young people that loved Jesus was incredible. The freedom there was at Fridays to get lost in worship and be challenged and grow as a young Christian was life changing.

It's hard, really, to summarise or pick out any specific stories from the many years of involvement with NYFC... there are so many good memories and servant-hearted individuals who mean a great deal to me and inspired me (and still do) to seek God's heart. Being encouraged as a young person to get involved, to volunteer and serve, while encountering an incredible and loving God who welcomed me, was immeasurably valuable.

The more I got involved, the more I found myself wanting to move outside of my comfort zone and try things I'd never normally do; from volunteering at an Arts festival in Poland for a few years, to painting during church services, learning to plan and lead at events and becoming part of the Fridays band. (Thank you to all, for enduring my enthusiastic djembe playing!) The joy of loving and singing to God with the rest of the band will always have a special place in my heart.

I sometimes yearn for those times again... perhaps it's an age thing? Life seems a wee bit more complex now than it did back then, and there's more grey (metaphorically and literal!) But learning that not everything is black and white, as it once felt, can only be a good thing. The wonder of God's unconditional acceptance and love is incomparable to anything we find elsewhere and that will never change. Yesterday, today and forever!

And Norwich YFC will always be a treasured part of my journey; a community of people that encouraged me to step outside of the boat and look to Jesus. That legacy remains and my faith and hope in God continues :)

My heartfelt thanks to one and all that I've known through NYFC. You're all history makers. For real.

Becky Kemp

Becs Wright

One of the best moments was when I was running a CU at a school. The children who came did not go to church, and would not have said that they had a faith. As time went on we had great conversations about life and faith and anything else they had in their minds. In the NYFC newsletter I asked for people to donate money so that I could buy them bibles. People responded and I was able to buy each child a bible. I had in my mind that they would be grateful... to be honest I was just hoping that they would be grateful and not reject them. When I gave them out, I have never seen a more grateful group of teenagers. They responded like I had given them a car each! I was so overwhelmed at their gratitude, I've never forgotten it.

Moments like this made working for NYFC amazing. The staff at NYFC made it double amazing! When I was pregnant and sick they made me a bed in the prayer room, so I could go nap...prayerfully of course!! They also were great to come back to after I had had a tough mentoring session at a school. Bringing in cookies, making me cups of tea, and making me laugh a lot!

Becs Wright

Ben Lawrence

Norwich Youth for Christ has been like that favourite pair of shoes you had when you were a kid, but had to throw out when your mum told you they had too many holes.

I first got involved with Youth for Christ in my teenage years, when the church I grew up in (Sprowston Methodist) employed a fresh-faced Luton Town fan called Paul Roast to be our youth worker. It soon became apparent that, other than football, Paul was very much into his music, which struck a note with me (pun intended).

My brother Dan, our best friend Dicky Baxter and I had started a band in our early teens. We would practise on Friday nights at the church. I'll never forget the first time we ever met Paul; he popped his head into our practice, told us who he was and proceeded to jam along on my spare guitar. A great introduction and - more importantly - a fantastic demonstration of what it looks like to meet young people where they are.

Over the years following, Paul worked with our group of odd bods and formed us into a team of friends, most of whom are still actively serving in churches across Norfolk. In the most unassuming way, Paul became a person that I looked up to immensely. He allowed me to grow in my relationship with Jesus and learn new things about music and leadership along the way. He also taught me some other less important things: how to speak Urdu, why no one plays guitar like Stevie Ray Vaughan, why Linux is the best Operating System and why Luton Town FC are (by his accounts) the greatest team of all time.

Naturally, I had to follow in his footsteps. So I signed up for a gap year at NYFC, went on to become a professional youth worker and ended up being Paul's colleague at twenty three - fulfilling the dream of an equally fresh-faced teenager. It's safe to say that I would not be where I am today without the influence and empowerment of Paul and many of the other NYFC leaders.

What does Norwich Youth for Christ mean to me? Well, it means change. Not just any change, but *positive* change. I would like to think that every NYFC employee or volunteer has had a positive impact on the lives of young people in Norwich. That is certainly true for me.

Youth for Christ is a movement that I am endlessly passionate about. I have experienced first-hand the positive change that can come through outstanding youth work. I love every moment I get to be creative, make wild ideas come to life and see young people's lives changed by Jesus. I regularly joke with the team here that nowhere else would let me get away with having so much fun - like that old pair of shoes, Norwich Youth For Christ is just the right fit for a creative being like me.

He also taught me some other less important things: how to speak Urdu, why no one plays guitar like Stevie Ray Vaughan, why Linux is the best Operating System and why Luton Town FC are by his accounts - the greatest team of all time.

Ben Lawrence

Beth Goymer

I am privileged to say that Youth for Christ have blessed my family for many years. With my Dad working for Norwich Youth For Christ in the late 80s and my Grandad being on the board for British Youth For Christ I was born into a family who were already flying the YFC flag years before I was.

I first experienced Norwich Youth for Christ at the age of 11 when I started to attend 'Fridays', a youth club that ran every other Friday and later changed to once a month. At Fridays, I got the chance to meet, pray and worship with other young people and receive teaching that challenged my faith and stayed with me throughout the weeks and years at secondary school and even today. The youth workers and volunteers were my role models displaying genuine care, true joy and a contagious love for Jesus. I still to this day have never willingly gone up to receive prayer like I used to on those Friday evenings. We spent the first part of the evening being entertained with the team's wacky ways of giving the notices (this on several occasions involved my older brother being volunteered to do something ridiculous!) We also played a range of wild and wonderful games that would occasionally push the health and safety line! The worship band led by Mark Tuma and Fliss Jones opened my eyes to a cool and contemporary worship style. They led with passion, sincerity and always pointed us Jesus. I can see how Fridays greatly influenced my walk with God and contributed to my discipline (at that time) to pray and read the bible.

I was fortunate that Fridays continued throughout my years at secondary school and when the time came for it to stop, I had already begun the next part of my involvement with Norwich Youth for Christ. It is hard to describe the love and community that I experienced at the gospel choir. Choir was a place you could come and get an injection of joy for the week. Everyone there, despite being so different (in age and faith) shared a love for singing but even if you weren't an enthusiastic singer the sense of belonging was too strong to turn down. I loved attending rehearsals and performing at various events and venues across Norfolk. I wasn't there long before a close friend of mine who had no church background asked if she could come along. She quickly became a committed member and continued to attend, even 2 years after I had left for university. She adored Fliss, Andy and Heather and could clearly see Gods love displayed in them. A year later, Norwich Youth for Christ took a group to Soul Survivor and she went along (thinking it was a choir thing!) and gave her life to Jesus on the final evening!

Throughout the years between this I have been privileged to volunteer at the choir, help lead a girls group, taken part in Hope 08 (my first experience of street evangelism!) and who can forget the first year we went to Soul Survivor in 2008 and won the talent show with God Has Smiled!? I cannot forget the biggest honour of serving as a trustee in 2015/6 alongside some wonderful, Christ devoted individuals who, like me shared a love and appreciation for all that Norwich Youth For Christ have done and continue to do today.

Beth Goymer (née Loaker)

Beth & Josh Mathieson

Josh and I joined NYFC Gospel choir in the summer of 2008. We didn't know each other. I, Beth, came from a Christian family and Josh was not. I had already been involved with NYFC through the summer outreach projects – REALITY and HOPE, I attended Fridays (a monthly youth worship night) every month and even did my work experience with them.

When I joined the choir I was too shy to sing, I eventually gave in and started to sing as an Alto. I was having trouble with friends at school and coming to choir was a wonderful mid-week break. Over the 3 years I was a member of choir I made wonderful friends, (most, if not all of whom I am still in regular contact with 4 years after leaving). I sang at gigs, went on mission trips, attended courses (like young leaders and girls/boys groups) and I can honestly say I gained another family.

Aside from the gospel choir, NYFC gave me small positions of leadership which have shaped who I am today. I helped lead girls groups and prayer groups, I went on to lead the icebreakers at Fridays and support in schools and after school groups. I have recently obtained my first graduate job in the arts and I was appointed because of my voluntary work and experience with young people. I would not have that experience had it not been for NYFC.

My life is all the better for the work of NYFC, I am a member of Church in Kingston upon Thames where I live with my wonderful husband Josh. We lead worship, an evening service and have just started an all age, all ability, no audition gospel choir! We would not be married, Christians or even half as happy as we are now had the amazing staff, trustees and supports of NYFC not invested so much into our lives. It is not just our lives; both my sister and brother went on to sing in the choir and now lead worship in their churches too! Thank you NYFC!

Beth Mathieson (née Miller)

I'm not sure I'd call myself a follower of Jesus without NYFC. I mean, I'm sure God would have grabbed me at some point, regardless, but at a time in my adolescence when I could either have gone one way or another, a friend invited me to 'some lunchtime choir at school'.

That led very quickly to dozens of amazing friends and the absolute highlight of my week. NYFC Gospel Choir gave me an experience of living *with* God and *for* Him, and set the foundations for the rest of my life.

Add to that, the fact that without NYFC and the choir I'd not have met my wife, and we're running out of reasons not to big them up!

Beth and I now run our very own gospel choir, as part of our church, and (though we're not a patch on Heather Land and the team), we've found something else to be the highlight of our week, and know better the God that is the highlight of our lives.

Josh Mathieson

Chris Starling

In the spring of 2011 NYFC took a group of young people to Poland to meet with the YFC team in Wroclaw and join in with ministering to the schools and youth groups in the area. I was very fortunate to be a part of this amazing team and I met so many amazing people on the trip.

Wioletta was the head of YFC in Poland and she would be our guide throughout the week. She had organised every day and had us visiting schools, conducting assemblies, teaching English, sharing our faith and exploring the sites. It was a great pleasure hearing the testimonies of so many people that we met.

I remember the first day there, the whole group was so tired it became difficult to distinguish between those praying and those nodding off!

This trip had a profound effect on me. It brought me out of my comfort zone and encouraged me to share my faith and my knowledge with complete strangers. I stood up and spoke to hundreds of children who were all hanging on to my words (or rather the translator's words!). A feat that I considered unthinkable just months before.

Most of the young people joining me on the trip were involved in the NYFC gospel choir which led to my fondest memory from the trip. Several memories in fact, as on many occasions Mark would bring out his guitar and we would all join together in worship, in people's homes, in the classroom and in the streets of Wroclaw.

The mission ended with the group splitting up and enjoying a meal at the houses of young people from Wioletta's youth group. It was such a privilege to enter into the homes of these wonderful people whom we had got to know over the few days we were there and it sealed the trip as a milestone in my life and one I hope never to forget.

Chris Starling

Clive Calver

One of the dangers with Youth for Christ lies in looking at it just for what is achieved under its own banner. For the whole story is so much bigger!

I was born in Ipswich, so as an East Anglian I certainly knew where Norwich was! Even if, as an Ipswich lad, I might have wished that I didn't!

Before Geoff Lawton and the dream that was to become Norwich YFC materialized, there were those of us who were YFC staff evangelists periodically working in the area. On one occasion I was there with musical pioneers Ishmael and Andy, and the guys were to do a concert in Norwich prison. I had to preach in a clerical collar (to prove we YFC evangelists really were Church workers). All seemed to go well, but I had been nervous and so used the toilet before leaving. Imagine my horror on exiting to see the two guys driving their van out of the prison gates without me! "Freedom" took on a new meaning that afternoon. So much for YFC friendship, collegiality and loyalty!

As well as links to the prison, Youth for Christ gave us connections with the University of East Angelia, located in Norwich. One weekend I had to lead a weekend away for the Christian Union in the University. Forty-five years later, feeling a little lost and sorry for myself in semi-retirement, I sat with a man in Capernaum, close to where my Jesus had once lived, to discover at that Norwich event those years ago I had led him to Jesus. You can imagine how encouraged I was, our God IS so good!

The schools visits, coffee bars, prayer times, church weekends, concerts, all were part of the thriving inter-church evangelistic ministry that NYFC created and operated. It was always fun to go there and be part of it. But, in 1981 I was asked to go to Nice, with two senior Church leaders, to ask Billy Graham if he would return to lead another mission in Britain? So the five centre campaign of Mission England was born.

But Britain had changed since Dr Graham's last visit. And the world's best known evangelist is renowned for his humility. He patiently listened to the heart cry that young people were ready to hear, and that youth evangelism was booming in parts of the U.K. Two direct results emerged. Tyneside and Norwich were two of the five selected venues, and at least 50% of the organizing committees were to be under forty years of age. These may sound small gains, until one looks at the age of accepted church leaders today, and the geographic redistribution of Christianity in the U.K. Much has changed!

All things have a beginning, and from NYFC an enormous amount has grown. My warmest congratulations go out to Nick Blanch and everyone involved today. May the seeds you sow today, produce a rich harvest tomorrow.

Rev Clive Calver

Daisy Palmer

I have loved volunteering with Norwich Youth for Christ over the last few years! I've enjoyed lots of great experiences such as going into schools to support youth groups, helping at Encounter, and playing guitar in 'The Jam' with an amazing team who have all helped to increase my self-confidence. I have grown a lot as a young Christian with the support of NYFC, especially in music! I absolutely love being involved with worship music – playing guitar and singing - and have been so excited about the Tracks van!

It was amazing to be asked to perform with my sister, Evie, at the Tracks Launch (September 2016) and although quite scary, it was such an exciting opportunity being recorded and interviewed by Mustard TV about the van and its function in encouraging young people to be creative! I'm so grateful that I have the NYFC team encouraging me with music progression and in my Christian life. I hope that these lovely people, and the gap year students I met, will be friends for life!

Daisy Palmer

Danny Ellero

In 2008 I took a gap year with East Norfolk Youth for Christ in Great Yarmouth. Part of my schedule included 2 days a week with Norwich Youth for Christ to ensure I was getting a broad experience. In Norwich my time was mainly spent with Paul in Hellesdon and Heather with the Gospel Choirs. After this, I did another gap year with Hope Church in Wymondham and again this was in partnership with NYFC. This meant I had an office base to work from as Hope didn't have a space at that time and it also meant I could continue to help with some of the projects and learn from the team.

My involvement in the two smaller choirs based in Poringland and Hethsersett meant I was able to work with them more on a personal basis. I could see them grow so much in their confidence and musical ability. Heather was very good at empowering others and encouraging them to step out and have a go. That empowerment and confidence was also in myself when she gave me the opportunity to lead the choir at a school concert.

A highlight for me was our performance at Norwich Cathedral. It was an amazing thing to be a part of. Our little choir could not only perform but it really was great quality and well received. It summed up what the choir was about, a small group of us making a big impact, seeing young people's lives changed through the simple act of singing.

As I look back, I realise how many life skills I learnt through this, including communication, time management, and how to plan ahead. But alongside the logical skills, there was always a spiritual edge. I remember how on one retreat, as a team, we read aloud the book of John together. It was a special moment for me, just hearing, resting and having God's word spoken over you.

NYFC was also where I met my future wife! Lauren was a young person of 15 when I first met her (purely platonic at this point!) but she had attended an event where the gospel choir were performing. She got involved in the choir as well and over time our friendship grew and by 2012 we were engaged! Lauren would also say that the gospel choir and involvement with NYFC helped to bring her faith alive. So we both have much to be grateful for.

NYFC has a continued dedication to always ensure that young people are growing in their faith. No matter what the project is, it's always at the forefront of what they do, to see them step up, grow and move forward. Both myself and Lauren are proof of this.

Danny Ellero

Dave Gallop

I first got involved with Norwich YFC through Fridays in the mid-nineties. My older sister went and on one occasion, I tagged along. I was really amazed at how different it was to how church services were and I was hooked. It was through YFC that I became aware of and was encouraged to try other youth focused events such as Soul Survivor and Living Waters – where at 16, I encountered the Holy Spirit and became a Christian.

NYFC were vital in providing further teaching and discipleship that helped instil a solid foundation of faith that I have taken into my adult life. Their staff offered programmes that were not provided by other organisations or churches and I have even continued to benefit from these into my thirties! (That's not 'youth', right?).

There are many trips, meetings and just 'times together' that I fondly remember and think of often. The camps I mentioned; Festival Manchester; Fridays; the Forum, ah - the sweet blessed pink pages of banter and real relationship building discussion. Withnail, Sparkles, frogprincess, Helsalata, Benvolio getting 'zeroed' for some minor infraction, someone being from Scunthorpe – Mark Tuma's blood pressure as we tried to find ways around the rules! I think the forum was truly a unique phenomenon, it happened before 'social media' and for me, really gave me a love of theological discourse - something that still *plagues* me today. But real understandings and opinions were formed and shared through that digital place.

NYFC are uniquely able and qualified to engage locally to compliment church initiatives and reach a specific audience. I am glad to be able to support their work now and encourage others to do so that they may continue to innovate and deliver to increasingly complex audiences.

Dave Gallop

David & Ann Adeney

It was a great privilege for me to be a Trustee of Norwich Youth for Christ from 2000 to 2011. During that time Norwich Youth for Christ changed, developed, moved offices and experienced highs and lows. A highlight for me personally was the gospel choir filling the Cathedral with praise and people, exceeding anything I had imagined.

Harder times centred around leadership and staffing issues, but in all of this I believe we, the trustees, were led to rely on the faithfulness of God. When we were faced with the need to appoint a new director in 2006 and had two remarkable internal candidates in Mark and Matt, against all my previous management experience, and the perceived wisdom, we believed we were guided by God to appoint two leaders. A wise and prayerful decision that led to a very real period of blessing.

I look back on my time of involvement with my fellow trustees, the staff and the work of Norwich Youth for Christ as a valuable time of learning and a greater realisation of the goodness and faithfulness of God.

"Your faithfulness continues through all generations." Psalm 119:90a.

David Adeney

I remember in the 1950s American servicemen from USAF Scunthorpe came in the name of Youth for Christ to Fakenham Grammar School showing Fact and Faith films. At the same time a young American evangelist, Billy Graham who had served on the staff of Youth for Christ in the States, came to England and through his ministry had a profound effect on the church in this country".... more examples of God's faithfulness and the beginnings of YFC in the area.

Ann Adeney

Dave & Linda Howes

We have great memories from the very start of NYFC, from the first committee meetings with Clive Calver and later with input from Eric Delve. The large gigs we ran packed with young people at St. Andrews with Graham Kendrick, Liberation Suite, Nutshell, Bryn Haworth, Sheila Walsh, Jamie Owens and others. You have probably never heard of most of these!

The fun we had constructing floats for the Lord Mayors procession - rooms full of balloons, hundreds of paper flowers and a papier-mâché two metre world! Our lawn covered in paint in prep for these. Also taking part in the Bishop's Youth Event at the cathedral with Cliff Richard, Cedars of Lebanon, and the Bishop's son Patrick who was part of the Ballet Rambert.

We also saw the bus project start up with Danny Pritchard before we left the committee in the early 80s. It was great being part of what God was doing, seeing Christian young people renewed and enlivened and seeing young people come to Christ.

Bless you in what you doing now as you continue reaching out to young people.

Dave and Linda Howes

David Sims

My walk with Jesus, as for many of us, has been full of highs, lows, and surprises. And it begins, also as many of yours does, with the ministry of Norwich Youth For Christ.

I started going to church in Great Yarmouth, and I didn't really understand much of what I heard or did - but something kept me going. One evening, the youth leader there invited me to an evangelistic event in Thorpe St Andrew High School, in Norwich, where J John presented the gospel to me. I heard all about Jesus, understood why he died for me, and was surrounded by people who were worshipping authentically and enthusiastically. I was rooted to the spot, before hearing God's voice (although I only recognised it was him later on!) inviting me forward to be prayed for. I remember being both surprised and affirmed when someone prayed with me there and then - and my journey began.

The church I was at, was fairly traditional and the vibrant worship I had experienced at the event enthralled me. So a few friends and I started to attend Fridays - a monthly event which offered contemporary worship, relevant teaching, and meeting young people who shared our faith. I remember making friends with Tazzy, Bob, Jam, and Mim - Hi guys, wherever you are! - as well as having strong friendships now with some people who were important to me at that time too. I remember some great debates on the online forum - and making some e-mates to share life's ups and downs with.

I am currently training to be a vicar in the CofE at Trinity College in Bristol - a story of God's colossal sense of humour. When I reflect back to my time at Fridays, it was these meetings which introduced me to a more charismatic style of worship, and a lifestyle which made working in the Holy Spirit normal - and these two aspects of my faith are the foundation to my walk with Jesus today.

To all the Friday's team - thank you. Thank you for the time you put in to Fridays, and all the other work you did. I doubt I would be where I am now if it wasn't for that J John event which you organised, and the Fridays which you offered. I often thank the Lord for you.

Come Holy Spirit!

David Sims

Edward de Kam

In 1997 YFC in the Netherlands started a Strategy process for the next 5 years. Local work in the Netherlands was in a big decline since the '80s and the few local centres left were working with one part timer each. It was difficult to survive and burnouts weren't uncommon. As a result of the strategy process we wanted to strengthen and renew our Local Ministry. Through our contacts with Richard Bromley from YFC UK we came in contact with Ian Savory from Norwich YFC. With a small team we decided to visit Norwich. It was an easy short flight and a warm welcome by Ian and his team. We were impressed and inspired. Having a disco with young people, being at a breakfast club for children at risk and an assembly at a school, being in their local centre with their staff and volunteers.

We had a lot of questions. How to work with a team of staff? How to fund all this? How to work locally with churches and schools together? We were impressed and inspired. They organized a lot of meetings for us. It ended in a McDonalds somewhere on the road meeting with Ian, Richard Bromley and Roy Crown. A great time with a lot of humour.

We had seen an example of how to build local work with a team. Back home, we made a plan to start 62 Local Centres in the cities with more than 50,000 inhabitants. Now about 20 years later we see great results in the local YFC work in the Netherlands. In the bigger cities, there are 16 local centres with Staff teams and volunteers. Plus, there are more than 60 smaller local centres and ministries with teams of volunteers - That's nearly 80 centres! But more importantly, so many young people found Jesus Christ through these local centres. It was a great stimulus for YFC in the Netherlands to reach young people in the urban areas, mostly far away from any contact with church. It is important to emphasize that Norwich YFC played a key-role in the start of this development to see it happen in reality. We are thankful for how the Lord blessed this work through your investment in the YFC Family. At that time we were not aware of the blessings to come.

"It is like a mustard seed, which is the smallest of all seeds on earth. [32] *Yet when planted, it grows and becomes the largest of all garden plants"* Mark 4:31 - 32a

Edward de Kam

YFC Europe, the Middle East, and North Africa Area Director

Ellie Hawke

NYFC was hugely important to me and really instrumental in my life during my teenage and young adult years. I was part of a village church with only one or two other teenagers so I found 'Fridays' such an encouragement, being together with so many other teenagers that loved God and wanted to grow in their faith. Looking back, the opportunities that were given us, to practise our gifts and take leadership in such a safe and gracious environment, being part of Fridays, S.O.G.I.T.s, and Christian Union leaders meetings was very key in my Christian growth.

It was during one Fridays meeting that I had an encounter with God that has really shaped my life and led me to where I am today. That evening I clearly felt God share some of His compassion for poor and abandoned children in the developing world and since that time I have mostly been involved in cross cultural missions in Latin America, Africa and now for the past three years in SE Asia.

I was also deeply impacted by the lives of the NYFC staff, particularly the way they invested in our lives, mentored us and sought to encourage us when they saw us pursuing the things of God. Margie Bone and Ian Savory in particular, spoke into my life at many points and gave me courage to follow God whole-heartedly and to pursue the plans He had for me. I remember one day sharing with someone at NYFC that I had an interest in politics and that perhaps I might pursue a career in politics so that I could speak up for the oppressed. A few days later Ian called me on the phone to say how excited he was that I had a desire to serve God in politics and really encouraged me to believe that if God called me He would open the doors. This kindness and interest in my life and my walk with God was hugely encouraging to me (though I didn't end up pursuing a career in politics… yet!). Though I am in my late 30's today, both Margie and Eric Bone and Ian Savory have not ceased to encourage me as I pursue God and his will for my life.

I am so grateful to NYFC for its many years of faithfully serving God through loving and investing in the lives of teens and young adults. I am sure there are thousands of stories to be told of lives massively impacted by the staff and programs they have run over the years.

Ellie Hawke (née Stubenbord)

Ellie Rodd

What does Norwich Youth for Christ mean to me? One thing that stands out for me is just friendship. I remember a group of us used to get 'that' 12 pack of Millie's cookies offer before gospel choir every Wednesday just to spend more time hanging out and doing fellowship… Yeah it was nice!

Girls group and Soul Survivor, Mission Academies and choir just really facilitated for me so many great friendships… like, life long friendships. I guess that's really important to me 'cause it's friendships rooted in faith and I'd never really had that before NYFC, so yeah, they're pretty great!

Thanks for doing what you do NYFC!

Ellie Rodd

Emma Craig

It's hard to put into words or quantify the impact Norwich YFC has had on my life.

I was a 'Fridays' girl. I had been told all my life I was a Christian but my family never went to church. I had started going to a local church but there were only 4 of us in the youth group. A friend heard of Fridays and we went along and never looked back!

Through this and other events Norwich YFC put on, I learned what it truly meant to have a relationship with Jesus. I learned what it meant to be part of God's family. I learned about friendship, dedication, commitment and fun! I made friends with people who I still call my close friends 18 years later (yikes!).

With all that I learned I went on to university with a clear sense of who I was and who I was in Christ. Without this, I don't think I would have made it through those years. People at the office put me in touch with Wearside and Tyneside YFC and I did some voluntary work with them. A specific talk from Ian Savory even led me to be tee-total throughout my entire time at uni as a witness to my fellow students. It also threaded into my university work - making documentaries about faith and so on. I also ended up being president of my Christian Union.

As life has moved on, I will always have to thank Norwich YFC for the time and effort invested in myself and my friends. It helped kick start my walk with Jesus and gave me the foundation with which to keep going, keep moving forward and keep learning about God.

Emma Craig (née Philpotts)

Eric Bone

Christmas Cracker Restaurant Project 1989

We first heard about this project at Spring Harvest 1989 when it was launched by Steve Chalke; the idea being to set up restaurants over the Christmas period, to be run by young people and to raise money for various third world charities. At the time, my wife Margie was a member of the Norwich Youth for Christ executive committee and I was an enthusiastic supporter of NYFC. (Margie went on later to become the NYFC Office Manager for 11 years).

We were stirred by the idea, thought it had great merit as a project and talked it over with Grantley Watkins, then the NYFC director. It would be fair to say it got off to a slow start. Grantley suggested we set up some talks at local churches, which we gave through the summer and early Autumn. At the first of these we got our first financial contribution (£2) from one of the young people who came along. Then in September, very much to our surprise, the Norwich Fire Service gave us a further gift of £250.

At this stage, our vision was pretty small – maybe we would be able to set up a four table restaurant somewhere, on church premises or maybe a small unoccupied tea shop. We'd need a few volunteers to run that, but we thought we could probably get them from our local church, or from young folks associated with NYFC. We had no idea what was just around the corner!

Our series of talks to local churches bore unexpected fruit. Late in September, I received a phone call from a Norwich Christian businessman, who told me that he had heard about the project, thought it was great, had just acquired the Bell Hotel for renovation and we could have the premises over the three weeks before Christmas. Well, after the shock was over, we said yes, probably the biggest leap of faith of our lives. For the Bell Hotel gave us the means of running a 100 seater restaurant and as a secondary source; a Tear Craft shop! We even had room for a non-alcoholic bar! The project had suddenly become about 10 times bigger than we thought.

There were of course a few obstacles. The Hotel had been gutted, was in urgent need of electrical repair and redecoration, we had no committed volunteers, no kitchen equipment, knives, forks, cups and plates, and at that stage no committed sources of food! We had about 8 weeks to get our act together. And Margie and I were both working full time. During that period, many miracles occurred. We turned building renovation over to Grantley, who found some truly amazing volunteers who worked sacrificially, for nothing, to lick the electricals and the decoration into shape. A good friend of ours who was a Tear Craft organiser took on the responsibility to the Tear Craft shop. Two other good friends took on the non-alcoholic bar. Margie took on the duty of recruiting and training volunteers and built up a team of over 70. Two other very good friends said "we'll set up and run the kitchen"; that was no joke, the kitchen needed a lot of cleaning and disinfecting before the equipment could be installed. And I took on the role of scrounger, for equipment and food, plus safeguarder of Health and Safety issues.

Somehow or other we managed to cram all of that preparatory work into the impossibly short period of time we had available. Included in the remarkable things which happened were the donation of as many potatoes as we needed (a farmer in Stoke Holy Cross), the donation of fresh bread every morning, the free loan of cookers, fridge freezers, and 120 sets of plates, cups and cutlery, from people with whom we had no previous contact. As the thing mushroomed and grew, and became better known, Grantley was in his element, being interviewed by press and local radio, forecasting scarily large benefits from the project (well they scared us). We even got, for free, the temporary installation of a security system to protect the £10,000 worth of equipment we had on loan.

Shortly before the restaurant opened, we held a special service of prayer and worship in the hotel, attended by many of the volunteers and other helpers, in which we thanked God for His amazing provision, and prayed for His blessing and protection over the time the restaurant was open.

The restaurant opened on time, with an "Oh Yea, Oh Yea" proclamation from the Town Crier, and we got off to a running start. Lots of customers on the first day, so many that we ran out of hot water from our temperamental boiler! But if anything the pace increased during the three weeks we were open. Maintaining standards was often a strain, but the volunteers all rose to the challenge splendidly. There was always enough to meet the daily needs, which turned out to be even bigger than we had thought. We even began running a few special celebration events in the evening for various local groups.

And when the event closed, the restaurant and bar had raised close to £18,000 and the Tear Craft store a little under £4,000. We said a very special thank you to all volunteers, arranged the return of everything borrowed, and Margie and I collapsed in a heap!

This was over 27 years ago, but the memories of that scary and fulfilling three months from October to December are still very vivid with me. Three things I am absolutely sure about. The first is that God was in charge of this project – we just had a tiger by the tail and ran with it. The second was the generosity of God's people in support. It was an ecumenical project; Catholics and Protestants worked and washed up together, there being no doctrinal concerns over simple acts of service. The third being that God can do infinitely more than we can dream of or imagine. Our simple image of four tables, and Grantley's (at the time) mad optimism in forecasting that £10,000 would be raised were just dwarfed by what actually happened.

To God be the glory.

Eric Bone

Fliss Jones

I remember sitting in my school assembly at Earlham High School. I was on the right hand side of the hall fairly near the front. There was an air of excitement and anticipation of what these visitors were going to do. It think it was 1992, I'm not exactly sure, but if so, I was 14. Norwich Youth for Christ had come in to my school to deliver Easter Unwrapped. I had been brought up in a Christian family and became a Christian at a very early age, although it only became clearer what that meant as I grew older. I've had many significant moments, 'God moments', that have shaped and defined my faith and relationship with Jesus over the years, and this day, at my school, was one of them.

The NYFC team were in my school. They were brilliant, dynamic, funny, captivating, and relevant and I remember feeling proud of my faith and this encouraged and inspired me to be bolder in declaring my faith in Jesus. As part of their presentation, they showed a video of Jesus dying on a cross, with the soundtrack behind it of 'Bryan Adams - Everything I do, I do it for you', which included the lyrics, "I'd die for you".... I can still remember 25 years on how poignant that moment was. Once the video had finished you could hear a pin drop in the school hall and that wasn't normal. I know that this message impacted every single kid and teacher in that school hall.... that moment in itself was precious, and I still pray today that that seed is in the hearts of all those young people, who are today heading towards their 40's, and every time they hear that song, it reminds them of a saviour who died for them. For me, it was also more than that, it was a significant, overwhelming moment of realisation that Jesus died for ME. I already knew that, but this was much, much more than a head knowledge thing, this was a HEART knowledge thing. Precious.

And NYFC have continued to play a MASSIVE part in my life. I loved going to all their events as a teenager. I was always challenged, inspired and encouraged in my faith and I have met lifelong friends. I got involved in their discipleship groups, and gradually got involved as a young leader. NYFC invested so much love and time into me, encouraging me in my giftings, helping me to discover my gifts and use them. I am SO grateful to them. I have been involved in Fridays, the worship teams, prayer ministry teams, Living Water teams, night club teams, core team, leading the intercession team, and more recently the Gospel Choir and have had countless opportunities given to me to serve and develop me.

I could write so much about this amazing life giving charity. Fast forward a few years, the opportunity to work for them as office manager came up, and in 2004, I started working for NYFC. I met (recruited!!) my husband, and we have been married 10 years and have 2 children. I pray my kids will find great youth work which inspires, encourages and invests in them when they get older.

I'm currently doing a coaching course at NYFC and one of the quotes from the course is that success is defined as knowing what God wants you to do and doing it! I feel my life is successful and that is nothing to do with my wealth, but EVERYTHING to do with discovering God's purpose for my life and living it out. NYFC have been instrumental in that. And now I get the opportunity to be part of the current NYFC team that are still going out and declaring who Jesus is, how much He loves us, and that He is hope and light and has plans and a purpose for everyone. I've had the privilege of seeing many young people grow into men and women of God, discovering their purpose and look forward to having the opportunity to invest into many more young lives. Thank you NYFC, thank you God.

Fliss Jones (née Scofield)

Gavin Calver

When I had the privilege of being the National Director of YFC I always loved hanging out with the incredible team in Norwich. They were innovative, Godly, compassionate and great fun. Every time a big personality moved on, you wondered what would happen to the ministry locally but each time the Lord bought someone else brilliant along too. The conveyor belt of youth ministry talent at Norwich YFC was seemingly endless!

I particularly remember speaking at a youth event in the Open venue (a former city bank) in early 2010. My wife was having a really complicated pregnancy and it was a time of great personal stress. I made the long journey along the A14 from Birmingham to Norwich on a Friday night to speak at the youth event. I was exhausted physically and spiritually but that night I prayed with three young lads as they came to faith for the first time. It reminded me once more why YFC exists and gave me a real spring in my step for facing the challenging going weeks ahead.

Keep up the great ministry Norwich YFC. May the best be yet to come!

Gavin Calver
Director of Mission
Evangelical Alliance

Geoff Lawton

The story of NYFC started well before Annie and I were married in 1975. A youth mission took place, under the name of Norwich Youth Evangelism, in the YMCA that backed out onto Bethel Street near to the city centre. Annie was one of the leading figures and Eric Delve was the evangelist. Many of the young people wanted to stay, worship, study and follow Jesus together so a youth outreach was formed called 'The Ark' and it met at the Julian Centre on Rouen Road. Some well-known national and local speakers were invited.

Desiring to be more evangelistic, Annie and I invited Clive Calver, the National Director of British YFC, to come and visit us. He came with Graham Kendrick and we asked why Youth for Christ was centred in London, the South and the Midlands with no presence in the east. We invited them to come to Norfolk.

They encouraged us to see it as a call from God to form Norwich Youth for Christ. Eric Delve, by now, was the National Evangelist for the movement and also supported our move. YFC began and was built on the work of 'The Ark' with various events including a series of concerts for young people in the hall in Cambridge Street off Unthank Road. We continued to invite well known speakers to events and many people came. We saw young people starting to follow Jesus and to serve and some of them we still have contact with. We had a great team of people helping us.

One of the best things we ever did was to form a Council of Reference of local church leaders. This gave us accountability and credibility with the both the church and other organisations including schools.

In 1979 I left teaching to become the first Director and schools worker for NYFC. The highlight of our tenure was the Down to Earth Mission which ran for a total of four weeks with three weeks in school and an overlapping three weeks of daily public meetings drawing the interest of local television and crowds of up to 1000. It was held, in what at the time was Delve's garage at the bottom of Rose Lane, and had to be covered with industrial polythene to stop the roof from leaking. Apart from Eric Delve speaking each night we had visits from other national leaders, musicians and the Riding Lights Theatre Company. What was really exciting was the number of different churches and denominations that came together, to work and to be part of it. We also had the wonderful encouragement of the then Bishop of Norwich, Maurice Wood. It was an extraordinary event with many turning to Jesus. Also at this time, Grantley Watkins became our second full time worker and when we left for London in 1984 he took over the leadership and developed it further in his own inimitable style.

Geoff Lawton

Graham James
Bishop of Norwich

I moved to Norwich at the end of 1999 so I've been Bishop of Norwich (and Patron of Norwich Youth for Christ) for almost half its entire life. What I love about Norwich Youth for Christ is the way in which it has adapted and reshaped its ministry to meet fresh needs and a rapidly changing culture.

When I first arrived in Norwich, NYFC was employing a night club chaplain. Tombland was then the centre of nightlife and I was walking along Tombland late one Friday evening when a small group of young people asked me if I was the nightclub vicar. (Everyone in a dog collar is a vicar but I assume they meant the chaplain.) I told them I was the Bishop. "You're not old enough to be the Bishop" came the flattering reply. Nearly 19 years on I certainly am! As it was it wasn't likely I was the nightclub vicar/chaplain since she was female.

NYFC has always wanted direct and immediate contact with young people. It's tried to always go where they are and connect with what they understand. That's why I was thrilled to bless TRACKS, the mobile recording and mixing studio. That night I recognised my technological incompetence. But what I had in common with the young people around me was a love of music, and especially music made in the service of the gospel. I expect more people have been converted by music – classical, gospel, choral, rock and pop when offered to God - than they have by sermons or books.

NYFC without music would be unthinkable. NYFC without praise would be unthinkable. NYFC without the churches of Norwich would be unthinkable too. One of the great encouragements of my time in Norwich has been the way in which NYFC has supported youth ministers and leaders within so many of our churches. It's had a great servant ministry helping to build up the Body of Christ in this city and extend God's Kingdom here.

I can remember my 40th birthday vividly. I wasn't too happy about it since it seemed to be the beginning of middle-age. I don't think it is with NYFC. It's as young as ever. Long may it remain so in the service of the gospel and of the young people of this city.

The Rt Revd Graham James
Bishop of Norwich
Patron of Norwich Youth for Christ

Hazel Erskine

I became a Christian when I was about 13. I am from Birmingham and I studied Geography at The University of Manchester from 2004-2007.

After graduation, I took part in a gap year with Christian Aid involving a lot of public speaking and leading youth groups across Norfolk, talking about Climate Change. I felt called to do this because God has given me a heart to fight injustice.

On arrival to Norwich in September 2007, not knowing anyone, I was made aware that my gap year placement would be split between Christian Aid and Norwich Youth for Christ. I was previously unaware of this and I was disappointed because it was not what I had signed up for.

My first week was spent on NYFC staff retreat in Cromer, with the team lead by the wise and humble Mark Tuma. We spent a whole day sharing and listening to each other's testimonies and I spoke my mind about being annoyed that my gap year placement was split with NYFC. I had never heard of YFC before so I had no idea what they were about.

Everyone kept joking saying "once you come to Norfolk, you'll never leave." I was adamant that I would escape but here I am...still living in Norwich...10 years later!

What was the reason I stayed? Well, on the first day, I met a very intriguing and mysterious young man sitting in the kitchen at the retreat venue in Cromer, wearing a red bandanna. I thought, "who wears bandannas these days?" As the months flew by and I had multiple opportunities to work with Chris Erskine and it became clear that we "liked" each other. I was petrified because I had always had extremely low self-esteem and confidence which I felt had prevented me from being who I wanted to be.

One year later, in September 2008, Chris and I started going out and in 2012 we got married. We had our first child, Elijah, in 2016.

My gap year was one of the most transformative years of my life for 4 reasons:

1) I had to trust in God in everything because I was terrified about public speaking and he honoured my prayers. I had prayed as a young teenager for God to give me confidence and he didn't disappoint. I was stretched to my limits but I gained such a sweet reward. My job now involves working directly with young people, running small groups and one-to-one sessions for MAP (Mancroft Advice Project). It's my dream job! I could not have gotten to this place without my experiences with NYFC and their prayers when I went to job interviews for youth worker positions.

2) I overcame my fears of falling in love with someone and fulfilled my heart's desire of becoming a wife and mother. I feel like God looked at our strengths and weaknesses and thought, "yes, they

would make a good team!" I'm excited about life with Chris as we endeavour to imitate Christ.

3) I fulfilled a personal goal of mine to sing a solo which was as part of the NYFC Gospel Choir led by the extremely talented Heather Land.

4) I have made some life-long friends at NYFC who are true legends, supporting and loving Chris, Elijah and I. I had so many laughs, a lot of fun and did a huge amount of learning.

Everyone who has ever been part of NYFC is never the same afterwards...we are better for the experiences God has given us.

Hazel Erskine (née Palmer)

Heather Land

Running the Gospel choir for NYFC from 2007 – 2013 was literally a dream come true for me – and I believe it was a God-given dream at that. Ever since leaving University in 2001, I had wanted to run a Gospel Choir. This was no doubt due to the fact that I had been involved in a Gospel Choir during my university years that had had a deep and lasting effect on me. Not only did I find great friendships through being in a choir, but they were friendships which nurtured me in the most wonderful way. I always say that I was 'loved back into the church', and this was predominantly through the Christian friends that I met through that choir.

Growing up I had attended church regularly until I was about 14, so I knew that God was there, but for some reason I hadn't received the Gospel in a way that was relevant to me at the time. In the weekly choir rehearsals I really took on board and thought about the lyrics that I was singing. I loved the songs and I found that Gospel music touched me and ministered to my heart in a very profound way, as well as just being such fun and uplifting music to sing! The songs we sang and the Christians I met of my own age in that choir played a pivotal role in me coming to know Jesus Christ as my personal Lord and Saviour.

I think I have just described where my passion and vision for working with young people in and around Norwich through gospel music came from!

I knew first hand that God could use a Gospel Choir to make Jesus known to people. And over the six years of running the NYFC Gospel Choir, myself and the amazing team of volunteers who helped me week in, week out to make rehearsals and concerts happen, witnessed many of the choir members come to faith in Jesus, or deepen their trust in Him. We also had massive amounts of fun in the process! Not only did we perform regularly together, but we went on residentials, and to Christian festivals such as Soul Survivor and Newday.

As well as seeing many young people exploring the Christian faith through the songs being sung and the witness of peers, the community element of being in a choir had other positive and transformative effects. It was a place of friendship, acceptance, and of celebrating each individual. We saw many young people increase in their confidence and self-esteem, as well as musicianship, and the no-audition policy meant that members could extend the invitation to join in to their friends. Over the six years we had over 200 members at different stages, and I love the fact that I still get to catch up with many of these wonderful people, as we have developed a yearly tradition of Christmas Carol busking, to raise money for NYFC!

It was incredible to see all the fruit that came as a result of starting the Gospel Choir project and I thank and praise God for all He did through it. The legacy of it includes so many great memories, friendships formed and lives changed, including mine. Thank you Jesus!

Heather Land (née Feltham)

Helen Roberts

Many years ago I had the privilege of being part of the Christian Union in Norwich City College studying at the same time that Margie Bone was doing a different course there. Little did I know that her friendship with me ran alongside her friendship with NYFC and very soon our paths were going to collide and my life changed for ever! One day I was 'summoned' by Ian Savoury to the NYFC office in their Oak-Grove-building. Going along to the meeting I tried to figure out what he might want to discuss with me – so I repented of all my sins (just in case) and guessed that he probably wanted to suggest I sign up for Operation Gideon. The conversation didn't go as I'd anticipated and instead of sending me off for a year Ian asked if I would join his team co-ordinating the Op Gid students who would be coming to Norwich. I've rarely suffered from being speechless but perhaps this was one such time. He sent me away to pray – always a good idea in such moments – and we arranged to meet again. Having completed my degree at the City College in Hospitality Management serving on the NYFC team was not the obvious next step. But it was what God had in His heart – and started a season in my life which I will forever be grateful for!

Ian was always one for good ideas – with the phenomenal ability to delegate much of the out workings to others! So when he had the idea for a musical to accompany the essential AGM it was me who was 'locked' in an office and not let out until I had written the script! Going into schools, youth clubs, prisons and nightclubs – were all part of the regular adventures. Dressing up became the norm although I'm still not sure how dressing up as nuns to help young people know that they were loved by Jesus really worked. And all of this in addition to journeying with some simply incredible Op Gid students.

I know I was there for a job and had a role to fulfil but to be honest what I took away from my time on the team will always supersede what I put in. Not because I was a slacker (in case you wonder) – but because the team were incredible! Over the three years Ian, and the team I had the privilege to work alongside, had a great impact on my life by what they said and did. I've got over the amount of blue-tac that John Loaker used to throw at me from his desk opposite mine and I've forgiven Ian for making me play my guitar and sing in the all-male prison – none of them had committed enough crime to really deserve listening to that!

I love that my history is hallmarked by NYFC and so much of what is going on in my life now, in my marriage and in ministry is the fruit of what was invested in me in Norwich '91-'94!

Thank you NYFC – happy anniversary!

Rev. Helen Roberts
Executive Minister
Wellspring Church

Ian Savory

Twelve years of working for NYFC and involvement with other YFC work for a further seven years. That's a long time for a DNA to get into your mind-set and shape how you look at things. The time in Norwich was a key time of fruitfulness in our own lives and in the lives of so many young people. So much so, that we are still enjoying the inheritance today, with many serving the Lord all over the world. In our lounge is a painting we had commissioned by a young local artist, Matt Gill. It was to remind me of the key lessons I had learned in those first 7 years in NYFC and to keep to the clear vision God gave.

Two key elements that were learned were;
1. You have to bring young people into the presence of God
2. No matter what you're thinking YFC is, 'a para -church,' 'missionary band', etc. etc. – discipleship has to happen! You can't be missional without it.

The NYFC staff always went to the YFC National Conference and on this particular occasion, Larry Lea was the key speaker. He spoke on The Lord's Prayer which transformed the prayer lives of John Loaker and I. As far as possible from that time, John & I would spend one hour, 5 days a week praying for the young people of the city. After a trial of praying in our own homes (this didn't work with small children around) the local vicar of St Mary Mags gave us a key and kindly allowed us to pray in the side chapel. This became our place of transformation because the moment we began praying for the young people, God began to show us more what needed doing in us and the lives of those young people. The picture God gave us was of a dirty beer glass – dirty on the inside – but where it was clean, that was God in us. Above the pint glass was a tap which was prayer that had started to flow through into us, filling us up from the inside. As the glass overflowed, God showed us sets of other glasses where the water (prayer) was flowing into – like a champagne fountain at a wedding. Each tier of the fountain became like the next move God wanted us to take. The key to this was us in God's presence making the difference. This is still true today for me as I have been relearning these lessons here in North Norfolk. The need for us to connect with Father, birthing thinking and vision in prayer is key to it being relevant and fruitful.

There were some significant events/projects which came out of this time. They were;

- Prayer & Toast – youth prayer meeting lasting 8 years seeing 20+ YP every week
- Bacon butty specials – larger prayer events
- FRIDAYS Community – Youth Church
- SOGIT's – Serious On God Intensive Training – developing young leaders
- Arena on Stage - bands
- Arena Takes Issue – debates
- Living Waters Event – following on from the very successful MAYDAY events @ Thorpe High School
- Nightclub Chaplains
- Connection Norwich Kids @Uni
- FRIDAYS House party – retreat weekends of training, worship & fun

The list goes on because imagination soaked in the presence of God leads us to the concept that where it's dark, that's where we should be putting the light on. This did, on occasions, bring conflict with churches, for example the concern that nightclub chaplaincy was leading people into worldliness.

One of the key layers for me was FRIDAYS. A community of Christian and other young people learning what it was to be disciples of Jesus, bringing in speakers such as Ross Paterson (Chinese Church Support Ministries) who encouraged many towards world mission.

At the first FRIDAYS there were about 28 young people and my first thought was that it wasn't going to last! How wrong I was! At its height there were between 180-200. The event lasted 13+ years.

The fruit is in the lives of the young people through strong relationships made during this time. The cost of commitment counted as one of the early phrases was "90% commitment is 10% short"! There was a strong desire to serve God wherever He led them. Seeing where these young people are now, as leaders who influence, blesses us constantly. There is never a month goes by where I don't bump into or meet up with Fridays young people, whether it's emails or comments on Facebook as to what impacted them during that time.

God be praised for all He has done and is continuing to do under Nick Blanch's leadership. God keep Nick in a place of radical discipleship.

At our commissioning service all those years ago Geoff Lawton, a founder NYFC director, gave us a word from God. This was it:

'If we are faithful here in this place, He would give us friends all over the earth'.

We are not really very widely travelled, but God has given us our inheritance in these young people as they change the nations!

Thankyou Lord!

For Christ & His Kingdom

Ian Savory
Senior Leader
Lighthouse Community Church

John Dade

I have been involved in various aspects of NYFC of which I will reflect on two. I joined the committee in February 1978 at its 'birth' and transition from 'The Ark'. My role was editor of the newsletter. No computers or email back then only a typewriter and plenty of Tippex! Progress meant moving from a manual to an electric typewriter. Illustrations were created by Giles Lloyd-Davies, a graphic design student at the Art School. We waited in anticipation for the first print only to see the errors we had missed during proof reading. We managed to raise a smile then during those early days of discovery. Giles was a brilliant illustrator but only after print did we notice his character beckoning people into the Ark had one thumb and six fingers.

These were exciting times. Twice we huddled into Geoff and Annie's front room as Eric Delve and National Director, Clive Calver, spelt out the purpose and vision of Youth for Christ. Clive explained how we were to host BYFC Touring events such as 'Evening for The King' and how strategic we were to the national picture. In terms of the Christian Youth Scene, Norwich was now coming on the map. Clive gave us an exclusive 'heads up' on a national teaching and training week that was to be held a year later at Pontins, North Wales later given the name 'Spring Harvest'. Some of us attended that rain soaked but positively memorable 'first of many' in 1979. Part of our medium term vision then was to release Geoff Lawton, then a school teacher, into full time work and ministry on behalf of NYFC. It was brilliant to be able to report in one of those early newsletters when this actually happened.

Being part of such an amazing bunch of people who formed this fledgling committee was a rewarding experience which would have consequences for me personally years later. I left NYFC for a while whilst the Newsletter progressed over the following years into a high quality publication thanks to the likes of Gabriel Swords.

In the early eighties I became involved in the music and worship aspect of NYFC initially under the leadership of Bob Lloyd and then taking responsibility of the worship band from around 1982 until January 1986. For the last few years of that time the band had a fairly consistent makeup with at its core Neil Bennetts on Piano, Alastair Groves on Guitar, Jenny Hayward (now Hall) on vocals, Malcolm Jackson on Bass, Andrew Southgate on Drums and myself Guitar, vocals and Worship lead. Two of these I still keep in contact with. Jenny and Neil who now live in Bristol and Cheltenham respectively. Neil Bennetts went on to write several worship songs and until recently led and oversaw the worship at New Wine.

After moving to Yorkshire I joined the Team at Harrogate YFC, funnily enough as news editor but before long was asked to be chairman. This period included appointing new full time director. My grounding and experience in Norwich had served well.

John Dade

John Loaker

A few of my favourite memories.

Prayer and Toast - For a number of years on a Thursday morning at 7.00 am we ran a prayer meeting followed by breakfast (toast). Young people along with Op Gids and others involved in YFC from across the city would come together before school to pray for revival. It was fantastic. Afterwards we would transport them to school - what a way to start the day.

What was really thrilling was to hear stories of some of these young people going onto university and other places and setting up their own prayer and toast meetings.

Summer Camps - every year for many years we had a summer camp. This usually involved taking over a school somewhere near the coast and having a mix of fun activities, bible study and celebrations. They were always great times of growth for the young people. The camp name developed into 'Camp the movie' for a number of years. We had some young people talented in drama who would write soap type sketches which would be performed by the YFC staff each night of the camp. I believe my name was Trevor in these. I still have the back drop sheet with 'Camp the movie' on it!! I have fun memories of these times with young people having encounters with Jesus which had lasting impact and also making and deepening friendships with each other.

As time went on the summer camps changed to become more mission orientated with each year the emphasis being on either evangelism or social action or both. I remember one year we split into groups with each group having a challenge to complete. One group had the challenge of putting on an old time musical show for the local old people's home and another to do an activity day for some disabled children. I can remember being very moved, seeing the creativity and energy put in to serve the community and the joy on the faces of those who attended.

Video roadshow - We developed a video roadshow called 'Action Replay', which we used to take into schools. It was a mix of crazy games and video clips through which we would share the gospel. We would often do schools weeks where we would go into the school and take lessons throughout the week, conduct lunchtime mini roadshows which would often be packed, and then do the full blown version on the Friday or Saturday night at the school. We would get good numbers to these and when we gave an appeal at the end would see many young people respond by coming forward to become Christians. I know these stories are meant to be all positive, but one of my regrets is not having an effective way to follow up on the decisions that were made at these roadshows. However it was thrilling to see young people's lives challenged with some of these coming through into the Discipleship activities of YFC.

East Anglia prayer walk - Grantley came up with the idea of walking around East Anglia and praying for God's Kingdom to come. In around 1990, for 4 weeks in the month of May, a core group and others who joined for different days or weeks, starting and finishing in Norwich, walked to various places, carrying banners, worshipping and praying. I remember it being very hot weather but a great time with a real sense of God's presence. I joined for the 3rd week with the walk finishing in Ely, my home town. We managed to take part in a service at Ely Cathedral and I was able to carry the banner down the aisle of the cathedral which I felt very proud of at the time.

There are many more stories to tell – *"Jesus did many other things as well. If every one of them were written down, I suppose that even the whole world would not have room for the books that would be written."* John 21 v 25

John Loaker

John McGinley

The simple truth is that I am sure that I would not be a Christian or in Christian ministry if it were not for Norwich YFC.

Having been brought up in a Christian home I began to push the boundaries of that faith when I attended secondary school and found the church I attended boring. When I was 12 in 1981 I attended the Down to Earth Mission that Geoff Lawton and others ran and remember feeling God calling me back to himself. It wasn't until 3 years later that I fully committed to following Jesus and YFC became the vital community for me to grow as a disciple.

I remember the YFC monthly celebrations at Dereham Road Baptist and Holy Trinity churches. Eventually I went on a YFC weekend away, I think at Letton Hall. I was struggling in my faith and cried out to God in one of those meetings. As Bev Smith, one of the YFC team, prayed for me I was filled with Holy Spirit for the first time – I didn't even know that this was what God was doing, all I knew was that I was transformed. As she prayed for me she prophesied that I would be a great man of God who would lead many people to know him. That word has shaped my life and sense of God's call.

I was soon involved in a small group that met in Colin and Bev Piper's house (with their dog Bignose!). There I learned to read and study the Bible, to exercise spiritual gifts and to have my first taste of leadership – they supported me as I helped to lead small group meetings, a Christian Union in my school, the Hewett Comprehensive School, and I remember them asking me to produce devotional materials for a summer week's holiday camp. It was a very significant time in which my faith and life were formed and grew. Since then I have been ordained as a minister in the Church of England, have led 3 different churches in which we have planted new congregations, seen hundreds of people come to faith and now have the privilege of being involved in the national leadership of New Wine, encouraging the renewal of churches and extension of God's kingdom across the nation.

Rev John McGinley

Vicar of Holy Trinity Church Leicester and New Wine Regional Director

Johny Grimwood

I was told these words could be serious or funny, but I could not choose! Working for NYFC was one of the most fun AND stressful AND rewarding times of my life (more on that later). I was a 'Fusion' community youth worker with Poringland Churches Together fifty percent of the time. The other fifty percent was as an 'office worker'. This incredibly loose term meant I dabbled in print/video design, internet stuff, event planning and being an event 'roady'. I was also a bit like Ralph from 'The Royle Family' sitcom. That lime-scale laden kettle was a trooper! I honestly can't imagine a more varied occupation. 7 years on I am volunteering as part of the youth team at CCC Attleborough.

The serious bit:

OK, so let me clarify, the stress bit was self-inflicted. I wrongly put too much pressure on myself to see results. Tangible evidence of lots of young people's lives changing for the better in Christ, instead of trusting in God that He will move in His time and His method. As a football fan I always looked forward to a game unfolding and seeing results. Being a Tractor Boy in a foreign county with a Canary (Matt Gooch) as a director made life interesting. I can only hope that I get to see what God has done with my scraps in eternity. I'm guessing He has used them somehow... He made mankind from dust after all. So if you work with youth, please bear this in mind and learn from my mistakes, trust lots and strive less.

The fun bit:

I will leave you with the most random moment I can remember. I will never forget the day I walked in to the office to get on top of the design to-do list. Top of the list was the new 'Fridays' (youth service event) flier for the coming term. In a moment of inspiration, Mark Tuma thought it was time Fridays shook off the dust and became more experimental (NB. Mark was also a director- He and Matt were like Ant and Dec- Buy one get one free). The design had to reflect risk taking but a photo was 'needed' on the front. About an hour later I remember entering a tennis court (near my house) being dressed in y-fronts, a vest, black wig and a top hat. I was 'advised' to perch myself on top of an amp trolley and let off an expired fire extinguisher while a sweaty Matt pushed me forwards. Mark did the gruelling bit and stood there grinning and taking photos. Some would say this is cruel to a new staff member and should only be reserved for stag do's. However I secretly enjoyed it and could not believe I was doing that for a job!

Johny Grimwood

Jonathan Richardson

While at Norwich School in 1983-84 we setup at school a Christian Union and although I lived well outside the city I was regularly invited to events run by Norwich YFC that my friends from the CU were attending. One of my most memorable was a barn dance in South Heigham Parochial Hall on Essex Street in Norwich – the Cumberland Square Eight baskets being a highlight. Another event was a weekend away at Letton Hall during the same period – three legged races up the servants staircase were something that I doubt would pass todays health and safety check! What I remember of these events was the way they brought young Christians together – for those of us living outside the city it was a revelation to find other young Christians to share time with.

For many years during the late 90's and early 00's we travelled up to Norwich with our youth group to attend Friday's firstly in St Albans Church on Grove Walk with Ian Savory and then later on Silver Street with both Ian and Mark Tuma. These events were a great way for us to introduce our church youth to a wider group of people – several of whom they discovered they knew from school. The logistics for us were difficult - having to travel up from Banham - and one memorable evening we managed to leave a young person behind! We usually insisted everyone came back in the car they arrived in so that we would know we had everyone – but this time we had a couple of people who had stayed in Norwich after school and wanted lifts home – and one car load refused to go back with the driver from the trip up! The danger of asking for volunteers from the church! All ended well and the team from Norwich YFC were great in sorting things out at the Norwich end while we contacted parents and arranged alternative lifts – not one to repeat!

Jonathan Richardson

Children, Youth and Families Development Officer

Diocese of Norwich

Josie from Brazil

Volunteering for NYFC in 2008 was an answer of prayer!

As an only child in Brazil, my future was quite planned for me. I was meant to be a lawyer just like many in my family. As soon as I graduated and told them I was going to work for NYFC for a year they disapproved saying it would take me years to pass the bar exam. But God wanted to show them that Mathew 6:33 is true and I passed it as soon as I came back, for HIS glory, miracle and testimony to my non-Christian family.

Looking back I see God moulding my path while working in NYFC alongside so many gifted people committed to Christ. He started teaching me to be intentional when it comes to loving and serving people in any context I´m placed in. Whether it was in the gospel choir, rock solid clubs, assemblies, kids clubs, coffee shops, prayer meetings, street pastors and all the activities aimed at relationship building and showing Jesus´s love and salvation. It helped me, despite all my limitations and failures, to find out how to live life for the kingdom no matter where He leads me.

I have now been working for 5 years in the law field. Looking back, I believe that the Lord allowed me to work full time in Norwich with young people as part of the plans He has me. Just like David danced and counted his blessing before the Arc of the Lord, I´m grateful and honoured for the time I got to work there and it´s in my bucket list to go back someday with my hubby and perhaps future kiddies! It was really fun and I have great memories!! Love to you all!!

Josie Archibald

Joy Clark

Having been brought up in a Christian home by wonderful godly parents; John & Pearl Breeze, who were heavily involved at Oak Grove Chapel where dad was on the eldership team, it will come as no surprise that I made a commitment to follow Jesus when I was 8 years old at a holiday club which my parents were helping to run at the church. I distinctly remember mum and dad's faith effecting our everyday lives, with devotions every morning over breakfast and lengthy discussions about the morning's sermon over Sunday lunch where dad would unpack the preacher's teaching and attempt to help me and my sisters understand what had been shared during the morning service. We asked many questions and were always curious to find out more!

However as a teenager, things changed and I began to struggle to live as a Christian, compromising my faith to fit in with friends at the grammar school I attended, whose outlook on life was very different to my own. Continuing to attend church I realised I was living a life with double standards and although they knew I was a Christian I found it hard to be a good witness to my peers.

In 1977 a new youth movement began in the city - Norwich Youth For Christ was being born and at 15 years of age it couldn't have started at a better time for me. I was at a crucial stage in my life: a formative season and one where I was questioning my own faith and making important decisions about my future and my life. I began to attend the monthly gatherings and really enjoyed the worship and teaching, learning songs that would never be considered in my own church where hymn singing was accompanied by the organist and nothing would interrupt the hymn prayer hymn sandwich!

Around this time I was also teaching myself guitar and so these new songs inspired me and allowed me to connect with God on a different level. Geoff and Annie Lawton were inspirational leaders and I also began to get to know Grantley and Flossie Watkins whose faith was also a real witness to me at this young age. These people were such fun and yet their relationship with God was really evident and their life and witness both challenged and inspired me to recommit my life to God, to live for him and grow deeper in my relationship with him.

One very memorable meeting I remember Geoff talking about living by faith. He shared about the fact that he and Annie didn't receive a salary in the same way that most people did and that he would pray to God for his needs as well as the needs of his family and the ministry of Youth For Christ. This made a massive impression on me as a young Christian, hearing the stories of God's miraculous provision time after time! Every time I went to one of the meetings my faith was challenged and I'd respond to God, wanting to live life like these amazing young men of God. Over the next 3 years my faith grew and I began to pray through serious choices about my future and prepared to go to London to study as a nurse, taking exams and courses which would eventually lead me to The Royal Free Hospital in Hampstead.

This wasn't the end of my association with NYFC and by now my younger sister Shelagh had begun to get involved with YFC as a volunteer and so each time I came home I would get involved with whatever was going on. In 1982, on one of these occasions, I returned home to discover a mission going on in the City. "Down to Earth" was making a big impact in the town and many people were attending the meetings and becoming Christians. Eric Delve and Roy Crowne were among the special guests that came to Mum & Dad's house where my sisters and I were roped in to help serve the hungry travellers! It was a great mission week and is still talked about today with fond memories of a time when God was really at work.

In November 1982 I returned home for another holiday to discover that once again NYFC was on the move and working in schools right across the area with a band called The Reps that toured the country at the invitation of churches and Christian organisations. Two of the lads from the band were staying with my parents and as I'd come home for a couple of weeks too, it gave me the opportunity to get to know them and find out more about their work.

One of the things I discovered was that these guys were visiting my old school on the Tuesday and would be setting up for assembly at 8am. Curious about what went on in a school environment and especially one like mine, which was so traditional and staid, I asked if I could come along! The assembly was a real eye-opener for me! Seeing this rock band playing to this crowded hall; to 1000 students who had all been expecting their normal hymn singing with gowned and serious head teachers leading it through, now enjoying something that was far more relevant to their culture and experience. I was so excited and inspired by what I saw. This experience was to make a massive and life changing impression on my life, something that I wouldn't be aware of until months down the line.

It was also this morning that I was introduced by one of our house guests to his mate in the band Andy Clark who played guitar and was also, I came to discover later, a great communicator and songwriter. Unbeknown to me - this encounter was to result in a huge change of direction for my life as I was later to meet up with Andy on subsequent occasions, eventually becoming his wife!

The rest of the week was filled with more schools work and evening events at youth clubs and churches and I was involved in as much as I could be, motivated by the impact that this band was having on the lives of the young people that they were meeting. Finally, Friday evening YFC put on the big gig and again I was involved with the prayer team. Chapelfield Methodist hosted the event and young people from all over Norwich streamed to this huge ancient building to hear the band! My youngest sister Ali and I remained in the prayer room throughout the concert with many others praying for souls to be saved, lives to be transformed and many to come to know the lifesaving power of Jesus! As the gospel appeal was given, over 60 young people streamed out to the prayer room to connect with local Christians who prayed with them and offered the opportunity for them to find out more at future meetings run by NYFC.

After many years of happy association with NYFC I was to also give up my regular salaried work to 'live by faith' as Geoff had so eloquently and passionately shared about all that time before. In January 1986 Andy and I would begin our own travelling ministry using music and testimony to share the good news of Jesus relevantly to young people all over the country. Now based in Rugby, our first booking was once again with great friend Grantley Watkins of Norwich Youth for Christ. Having heard of our intention to step out in faith as a new duo called "DOUBLE CHECK", invited us to Letton Hall to lead worship for the gathered youth workers that were away on retreat. He was really keen for them to get to know us and find out about the work that we were doing. I really believe that this was the foundation that prepared us for 30 years of ministry. A bunch of youth workers that then booked us to visit their churches and schools over the next 12 months that would allow people to discover who we are and what we could offer. The diary filled up off the back of that weekend and we've never been short of work since that day!

Now working for British Youth for Christ, we also invest in young musicians to do the same and over the past 17 years have worked with 50 gap year volunteers enabling them to reach young people too. Our affiliation with NYFC continues and we are consistently inspired by their unique and innovative projects used to reach young people in the name of Jesus and we look forward to an ongoing relationship as we partner with them through mission and events in the years to come.

Joy Clarke

The Sense and *Stance* Team Leader

Youth for Christ

Norwich Youth for Christ first logo

SPRING 1979
ARK NEWS
NORWICH
YOUTH FOR CHRIST

Lord Mayors Procession 1979 – Norwich Youth for Christ were regularly involved in the procession.

First Down to Earth Mission – Delve's Garage - Clearing up the space where it is to happen – 1981. Many people came and heard the gospel message resulting in giving their lives to Jesus.

Down to Earth Venue – Once renovated

Director Geoff Lawton, Eric Delve and the Bishop of Norwich, the Rt. Rev. Maurice Wood.

City Serve 1992 – read all about it!

Eastern Daily Press, Saturday, August 15, 1992

CHURCH NEWS

Meeting challenges

Young Christians in action to help others

A pioneering project called City Serve has been hailed a great success by its organisers, Norwich Youth For Christ.

A group of 47 young people aged between 13 and 20 spent a week at the Blyth Jex School, meeting challenges set for them to help groups of elderly people and others with special needs.

"We were absolutely thrilled to bits," said Margaret Bone, of NYFC.

Youngsters were put into teams and assigned one of five projects for which they had only a couple of days to prepare.

Some of them were asked to provide entertainment for children with special needs at the Thorpe Hamlet Centre; another group organised a barbecue, disco and fairground entertainment for a party of adults with special needs; others visited a John Groom's Association centre for the disabled with a barbecue and quiz evening; another group was responsible for an old time music-hall for a group of elderly people from the Rosebery Road Methodist Church Over-60s Club.

Apart from their challenges, the City Serve team visited elderly people and did household chores or ran errands for them and undertook gardening at the Hebron House drug rehabilitation centre.

NYFC would like to hear from anyone who would be interested in being involved in any future projects of a similar nature. NYFC can be contacted at 70, Catton Grove Road, Norwich (Norwich 415756).

■ If you have an item of news you would like us to consider for this column, please write, giving as many details as possible, to: Andy Bash, Church Chat, Eastern Daily Press, Prospect House, Rouen Road, Norwich, NR1 1RE. Remember to include day and evening telephone numbers.

City Serve: working together to help others.

March for Jesus

Worship has always played a big part in our outreach

Staff worker Simon Kirby and Director Ian Savory looking fresh faced 1993

Norwich Youth for Christ staff, volunteers and young people around 1993 / 94

Roy Crowne giving the 'sex' talk! Every good youth worker does this at some point!

Young Leaders course praying over our city – around 1994 / 95

Blood of the Lamb performance – 1999 – Ian Savory, Director, loved to put on a great show!

Our club work ministry started in 1993 under staff worker Tracey Hyslop and continued for over 10 years.

Supernova – 1998 – A special club night run by Norwich Youth for Christ in a local nightclub on a Sunday evening for young people to come an experience a club night in a safe, non-alcohol, environment.

Rock Solid Training with staff worker Tim Yau around 2000

J John at our Just 10 envisioning event

Norwich Youth for Christ taking a lesson in a local high school. We love doing lessons!

More Schools work

Christmas Unwrapped – 2000 – Staff workers Matt Gooch, Mark Tuma, Tim Yau and volunteers taking the Christmas story into schools. We love of our history of creatively delivering the Christmas and Easter message in schools over the years.

Ronnies youth club - One of our projects with a partner church. Pictured Staff worker Matt Gooch, Church Leader Rev. Andrew Tyler, and the Bishop of Norwich – 2003.

Using a double decker bus to do youth work has been a big part of our story. Here, staff worker Matt Gooch runs the Bus Project – A mobile youth club venue reaching kids in rural locations.

Here are two of our previous staff workers, Bex Wright and Paul Roast dressed up ready to deliver a holiday club and youth event. It is not uncommon to see a staff worker 'in costume' ready to deliver anything from an assembly to a youth service.

They are following in the footststeps of those gone before…..

Grantley Watkins, Paul Cracknell, Ian Savory and Geoff Lawton – all previous Norwich Youth for Christ Directors – celebrating our 25th birthday.

The Mix at Living Water 2006. We have had contact with 100's of young people attending our programmes at Living Water over the years and seen God do significant things.

Staff worker Johny Grimwood – Youth work at its best. Photoshoot for Experimental Fridays. 2007.

Speaking of Fridays, here's a picture from the 90's. It ran for almost 20 years and we still hear testimonies today of what God did through Fridays.

After a sucessful Reality Event, we did Reality II in 2007. Young people gathered to worship and receive teaching in the morning and in the afternoon we sent them to various locations in the City to run kids event, do social action and be a positve influence in the community.

We have had many Gap Year Students over the history of Norwich Youth for Christ. We love to watch them grow over their year with us and see how God uses them in the years to come. Here are two of our Gappers from the affectionately known 'team Stoff' in 2010 with Director Mark Tuma recording for our new pod cast project In 2010.

The Norwich Youth for Christ Gospel Choir at their amazing Norwich Cathedral concert in 2010 where they launched their first CD 'God Has Smiled'.

We have taken many grous of young people to Soul Survivor. In the 90's our young people served at the event running Café Uno. This picture was in 2011…. The year our coach was not big enough to take all the luggage!

Norwich Youth for Christ Gospel Choir at Soul Survivor and win bandstand competition - 2008

Our links with Poland Youth for Christ began way back in 1989 and we have been supporting them ever since. This photo was taken in 2011 when we took a group of young people mainly from the gospel choir to do mission work.

Residentials are another key part of our work creating opportunities to deepen relationships, learn new skills and do more youth work and disciplship in a weekend than you can in 6 months. This is a trip to Hostead around 2010.

Neway is a summer camp right on our door step. No coaches needed, just lots of energy to make it through this week long event. It's all worth it to see the outcomes of taking young people to these events. Picture taken in 2012

TRACKS VAN launch. 2016. Another dream, another vision realised, another pioneering project led by staff worker Sarah Ballard to continue to help us bring Good News to young people, with our multi media, recording studio Tracks Van.

Now in 2018, some of our most recent work, along side TRACKS, is our music and media projects. Here is staff worker Ben Lawrence working on a film project.

Karen Coleman

I remember it clearly. Peter Barnes stood at the front of Dereham Road Baptist Church and said NYFC were advertising a job and he felt someone in the room could do the job. My husband nudged me in the side. At the time I was a store manager for Woolworths and only just beginning to think that the job was not something I could do till retirement! The next day I called Paul Cracknell and had a long conversation about the job. Very quickly it seemed I was in post as the Office Manager. As if to confirm I had done the right thing, the Sunday before I started the service leader at DRBC, Sue Seeley, asked me to give a testimony on what God was doing in my life. She had no idea I was about to change careers. God had confirmed to me this was the right thing I was doing.

Working for NYFC was a spiritually stretching experience for me. After the first few weeks I thought 'how do these people pay the staff', because there was so little regular income. I had only ever worked for big firms and I had not grown up in a Christian family where these things might be talked about. However, for all but one month we got our salaries on time. The one month was definitely challenging but thankfully we were blessed with Trustees who took their part in NYFC seriously and ensured the staff were cared for. There were times that we prayed as a team at 12 noon each day when things were tough and watched God provide.

Our staff times together helped me immensely in my growth as a Christian: Praying regularly for each other, the young people and the ministry, and watching what God would do next. I had not been exposed to much that would be described as charismatic in the church and working at NYFC gave me a taste of how God works today and I have wanted more ever since. I wish I had kept a record of the times cheques had arrived to provide for our needs at just the right time, but this is something I learned later.

The sense of team is a strong feature at NYFC and I have to say I still miss it very much. The willingness to look out for each other meant a great deal to me.

When the time came to leave, Andrew's job took us to Northamptonshire, I naturally wondered who might be next. I knew of Fliss, who had been a key volunteer for the team for a long time. When Fliss came to talk to me about the job I had one of those moments when your stomach does some sort of God flip and knew this was the person for the next season. It was very exciting when the Trustees appointed Fliss as the next Office Manager and the rest as they say is history.

God bless NYFC and may the ministry flourish for many more years.

Karen Coleman

Katie Clough

I attended Framingham Earl High School where Norwich Youth for Christ worker, Heather, was running a small gospel choir after school. My sister had been going along so I wanted to join. I only went for the singing! But from there I joined the larger city centre gospel choir. There were around 30 other young people there but it was very welcoming and I quickly made friends.

As a group we would visit churches and sing at their services - again, I went just for the singing! But while I was there I was listening to what was being said in the church services and it was sinking in. We visited a diverse mix of churches and I kept hearing about God. I always liked the community feel in churches but I didn't get the God stuff.

Then NYFC organised a group to attend the youth worship camp, Newday. I just went because my friends went but this was the time then I started to know Jesus more personally. I could see other people my own age having a personal relationship with God. I wanted that so it was about being open to God and letting Him do the rest.

It suddenly made the choir seem more relevant, the songs stood out more. After choir sessions, they were doing bible studies and I stayed after and joined in with this too. I started meeting with Heather and Fliss regularly, to chat more about my new found faith. But around this time, my Mum got ill with cancer. I went to choir the day I found out. There was a prayer meeting before choir and I arrived and just cried. I spent most of that choir session crying with Fliss.

So now I was exploring my faith in light of illness and suffering at a very personal level. How do you understand that God is good when your mum is on life support in hospital?

I also got involved in some of the NYFC projects in Poringland with Johnny and Pete. This included an after school club which was an introduction to faith with different topics and then another club for those who wanted to go deeper. All of these things gave me the space to explore and ask questions without being judged. Through this I also found Christians in school that I could make friends with. These friendships gave us a link into church and I started to attend Kings Norwich.

Then the choir had a booking to sing at Hope Church in Wymondham. It was a baptism service and the offer went out to the choir - If anyone wants to get baptised, the church was happy to do this. Three days before, I decided to go for it! Heather and Fliss met up with me to ensure I understood what it meant and they baptised me on the Sunday! Despite the short notice - my parents and wider family also came along!

Sadly when I 19, my mum passed away. I still find the questions around suffering and God's love difficult, but in the end, mum's passing was the end of her suffering. There are lots of things that I'm grateful for too. Mum looked like she would die when I was 14 but she survived for 5 more years. I believe that this wouldn't have happened without God. When we recorded the gospel choir cd, mum would listen to the cd on repeat in hospital after her first major operation. In her will she wanted one of the songs played at the funeral. I find this helpful, knowing that by being in the choir, it helped her.

God also gave me the strength to do things that I didn't think were possible. During her illness, there were times when I had to go home at lunchtime to make sure she was ok and had taken her medication. Even times when I had to wash and dress my mum. I was able to do these things and still pass my A levels. It wouldn't have been possible without God.

And God has always given me people, whether NYFC (especially Fliss!) or church youthworkers. I am grateful for the people he has put in my life, helping me to process and walk through it all. I'm still working through the loss of my mum and I think it will be a long process but He has enabled me to carry on and lead a (fairly!) normal life.

Katie Clough

Katrina Harper

NYFC invited me into their huge family when I joined the Gospel Choir in 2009. Being in the first couple of years of High School I was trying to figure out my identity, seeking deep friendship with my peers while attempting to strengthen my relationship with God. Looking back I see how during these fragile years, I was strengthened so much by this amazing family. I made multiple lasting friendships. It gave me confidence to use my voice to glorify God and in this it encouraged me in my relationship with Him. Just the other day I was listening to Kirk Franklin and reflecting on the songs we would sing together as a choir and the power that's portrayed through united worship and song - and the harmonies would always just sound awesome! I was also a part of the girls group lead by Heather and although there were only ever three or four of us who went along, I was continually challenged through what we studied, and those girls are still my best friends to this day!

At some point I got to be a part of the Growing Young Leaders course. This gave me confidence, a few years later, to join Youth With a Mission (YWAM), take part in their discipleship program and eventually go on to staff it!

God moves in mysterious ways as since then I have got married and my husband and I are now living for Jesus in the Himalayas. Our hearts are daily being stirred more and more for discipleship and training others into salvation and in their own walk with God. I am grateful for every seed that NYFC planted in me and am amazed at how the things God spoke to me about back then are still unravelling into new opportunities today.

Katrina Harper (née Taylor)

Keith Willers

I had the privilege of volunteering for NYFC for ten years. It started as an opening in the Fridays' worship band which I found very fulfilling. I had the opportunity to help lead people in worship and also be part of helping to organise the Friday' fortnightly youth event. This took me to many places spiritually and also physically and I have very fond memories of it.

But out of the Fridays meetings and all the one-off events i helped out at, the most value I feel I gained was through something I hadn't expected and it only became apparent to me many years after it ended. I was involved with the nightclub work in Ritzys/IKON nightclub with Tracey Hyslop helping clean people up after they spewed their guts up through substance misuse, administering first aid, taking people to places of safety, or just being a friend and a listening ear. NYFC's work in that night club built true community. Little did I know how much the impact of the regular volunteering i did in that nightclub would have such a profound effect on my life. The lessons I learned, skills I discovered I had and new things I learnt about myself and others had such an effect on me that God has used that to take me into working full time with the homeless people of Norwich for ten years now. That is something I would never have planned to happen but I guess God did!

I thank Him for these experiences and look back in hindsight and am able to see why He put me in that place at those times. I would not be the person I am now without these experiences and I am grateful to NYFC for providing the platform for this to happen. It was also an amazing amount of fun and I met some incredible people.

Keith Willers

Lauren Ellero

In 2008, in my final year at high school and Heather's first gospel choir session at Hethersett High School, I went to my first ever gospel choir rehearsal. I absolutely loved it and knew it was a way in which I could explore expressing my faith through my love of music. I was made to feel so welcome by Heather and realised that she wasn't just there for the music but because she cared about me and my life. I was so sad when I reached the end of my final year, I knew it would mean leaving the gospel choir and all of the relationships I had built while I was there. Heather had invited me to the Norwich choir but I wasn't sure how I would feel going along on my own to an established choir. The encouragement was wonderful from Heather and after a difficult summer, I knew that choir was the best place to be.

I will never forget my first rehearsal at NYFC Gospel Choir. I walked to the venue wondering what it was going to be like, whether anyone would talk to me and what other Christian young people looked like, as there hadn't been many in my church and the ones I did know had let me down. I followed two young people through Norwich, not knowing where they were heading and amazingly they also walked all the way to choir (of course God already knew!). I went home that evening not being able to stop talking about how incredible choir was. I talked about how friendly everyone was, how they had welcomed me, the music we had sung, the awakening of my soul that I felt and how I wanted to go again already! It became the highlight of my week and I finally felt like there was somewhere I belonged.

One rehearsal, Andy turned to me and had felt God say that he needed to ask me if I liked working with children. I loved working with children and wanted to be a primary school teacher (which I now am!) so I started helping at a kid's club and holiday club with him in Wymondham. That's when I started attending Hope Community Church in Wymondham and I recommitted my life to Jesus on the Kid's Weekend Away in May 2010. I had realised that through the love, care and acceptance that people at NYFC and church had shown, that there was more to my relationship with God than I had known, that somehow the gift of music that God had given me, gave me so much more than I could've imagined. My favourite times were immersing myself in our Gospel music in praise to God whether that be at different churches on Sundays, recording albums or in our amazing concerts. We had a purpose in sharing the love and grace of Jesus through the love and community of our Gospel choir family.

I also met my now husband through the time I spent with NYFC Gospel Choir. Danny and I became friends when I first started in the Gospel choir, and we got to know each other through the way that we all shared our lives with each other and journeyed through our faith together. A couple of years later, we knew that God had more planned for us and in July 2014, we got married and started our marriage the way we wanted to by leading worship at our wedding! We are both now members of Hope Community Church and lead worship together regularly, our life is rooted around our love of music and our devotion to Jesus.

The memories I hold from my days in the choir are so precious to me and it's a chapter of my life that I know has made me the person I am today, the person who God wanted me to be. I have made incredible friends for life and I love journeying through my faith with such special people. I will forever be thankful to God for the amazing work of everyone at NYFC, especially Heather, and the sense of belonging, purpose and direction He brought to my life through the Gospel choir!

Lauren Ellero

Margaret Smith

I think I must have been involved with NYFC for over a quarter of a century – how time flies! My early recollections were of Council of Reference meetings (never did quite get hold of what they were about!), meetings at Oak Grove Chapel going up flights of stairs and having coffee and cake as we talked (!), being taken out to lunch by Peter Nicholls, the then chair of Trustees and inveigled into becoming a trustee (and being alarmed that, with finances then in a very precarious state I would end up having to sell our house to cover NYFC debts!).

I well remember the excitement when the office moved into the city, to the CEYMS building on the Debenhams site – up 78 stairs! Everything went up those 78 stairs – paper stocks, equipment, staff, volunteers and trustees. I recall the notices on the stairs – "Only another 4 to go!" and wondering if my heart would give out before my legs! I remember the bliss of moving to our current building in St Giles Street with reduced stairs and vast office space. Amazing, though, how vast space creates stuff to fill it!

I recall emergency Trustee meetings looking at loans to cover salaries when funds were very low – and how God always provided, sometimes at the last minute but always by his grace so that redundancies never happened.

Now I find myself as Chair of Trustees, looking back with gratitude to God's provision and leading, looking back with gratitude for the many youth workers, volunteers, trustees and directors with whom I have shared in this ministry, looking forward to all that God has planned for this wonderful, vibrant organisation that is Norwich Youth For Christ, and feeling humbled to have been just a small part of it. It's been a privilege to see the lives of young people changed by the power of the Cross of Jesus Christ - to Him be all the glory!

Margaret Smith

Chair of Trustees

Norwich Youth for Christ

Mark Tuma

I had never heard of YFC before I came across Norwich Youth for Christ. I hadn't been a Christian for very long before coming to Norwich back in 1992, only a few months really. I was in my second year of UEA and NYFC had their Annual Thanksgiving, with special guests London Community Gospel Choir. Naomi (Tuma) told me that they needed some amplifiers for the band and as I had a bass amp I offered it up. Naomi told me that I had better be at the event and listen to them! I don't think I had any particular expectation for the evening or knew anyone on the team back then.

The Annual Thanksgiving was at the Salvation Army Citadel and it was packed! It was a good evening but it was really when Ian spoke that it grabbed me. He spoke about the heart and vision of NYFC with his usual raw and honest passion.

I went up to him at the end and said, "What can I do?" Over the following weeks we got chatting and it resulted in doing a gap year with them. My time was mainly on the Heartsease estate doing detached work and helping with a community youth club. The kids we were engaging with were from difficult backgrounds and we had a variety of responses, but I really enjoyed it. After that, I took a job in engineering and my assumption was that this was my career path.

But two years later, on a random evening, Ian Savory turned up on my doorstep completely unannounced and unexpected. It was

9.30pm, straight after a trustees meeting and he said, "We've been thinking - do you want to work for us?" It was completely out of the blue and I wasn't looking for anything else at the time. But the role (for a bus ministry) didn't seem like a good fit so I said no. He came back a few days later and said 'What about this then?' The new offer was looking after the gap year team. I could see myself in this role and it seemed like God was nudging me so I handed in my notice at my engineering firm and took the job!

Over my time with NYFC I had a number of roles that spanned nearly 15 years. But there was always an overall narrative there that boiled down to a desire to see people understand who they are in God, what He has made them for, how much He loves them and what He has called them into. Once they understand this, they can grow into the potential of who God has made them to be and they can teach other people those same truths.

This happened when I worked with young people, when I oversaw the gap years and even as the Director when my focus was on the staff. The most exciting times for me were when the lightbulb moments came on and people got it and understood it and then went on and did something with it.

Before I left, one of the last events I spoke at, was at the South Norfolk camp by Integrate YFC at Sizewell Hall where there were 30-40 young people attending. Most of them were unchurched and I realised I had three or four days of talks to give and they were all coming in with no prior Christian knowledge. So we planned to build up the teaching gradually to the penultimate night where there is an opportunity to become a Christian. But it didn't happen like that because on the first night, pretty much everybody said 'I want to become a Christian'. That was brilliant! But it shows that our plans are not as good as God's plans. Sometimes we are afraid to ask and give opportunities because we think they won't be interested or ready. But people are more ready than we think and God is doing things in more ways than we expect.

Looking back, it was a blessing and a privilege to be involved. There's nothing special about me. If you were going to grade people based on Christian score system, I wouldn't score highly. There is nothing that makes me more qualified than anyone else to any role at NYFC. It's just God's blessing and privilege that I got to do those things. I'm very grateful for that. I'm also really grateful that the organisation exists and existed because I felt that we were able to do things that others weren't able to do. We were able to pioneer in places that others couldn't pioneer in and able to do things that united where others couldn't unite. Because of that, there are people whose lives are touched by God now who wouldn't have been touched otherwise. And that is pretty amazing.

Mark Tuma

Martin Forster

The origins of Norwich Youth for Christ....Maybe!

I say 'maybe' because things happened a long time ago, and events seem to merge together. But to begin with I certainly remember Geoff and Annie Lawton starting a bible study group on Thursday evenings at the small hall beside the Julian convent on Rouen Road. This was in 1976 (I think) - maybe you came along too?

We soon grew and began holding monthly Saturday night meetings for everyone where we invited various people to speak. Roger Forster and Tom Rees came to us, and other speakers from around Norwich too. On more than one occasion we were joined by a popular Christian group, 'Nutshell' (remember them?) who came to sing for us. Evenings like these proved very popular and before long we were running out of space in the small hall. I don't recall how long we'd spent there but we left Rouen Road and began to meet at St Mary Magdalene on Silver Road and I know that much later we also used Holy Trinity Hall on Cambridge Street.

Our next move was to become the ARK fellowship. We had our own newsletter produced by John Dade, with wonderful artwork by Giles on the front cover (existing copies must be worth a fortune!). The Ark Fellowship then led on to us becoming a British Youth for Christ centre, with Geoff Lawton as our first director.

I'm sure that some of this 'evidence' wouldn't stand up in court and that some of you 'oldies' will remember things perhaps differently, but we can all agree that God has been faithful and prospered the work that was started all those years ago. Here's to the next forty years for Norwich Youth for Christ!

Martin Forster

Naomi Tate

I got to know Norwich Youth for Christ at a really rubbish time in my life. I was so angry at God and I didn't really want anything to do with Christians. But I did love singing!

When I heard about gospel choir I just had to give it a try and I fell in love! It was unlike anything I had known before, it became more about the friends I was making and less about the fact there might be Christians there; they accepted me anyway. Gospel choir was the highlight of my week. It became obvious pretty quickly that things weren't ok with me. Heather, who ran the gospel choir, pulled me aside one day and asked me if I would like to go to a bible study she ran with Youth for Christ. I started going and ended up learning a lot about God's nature, He didn't hate me for anything I'd done, He still loved me!

Heather was the most amazing example of this love for me. She would sit and mentor me and give me little jobs in the office to keep me occupied and on the bad days she would pray. Through this mentoring and Heather's obvious love for God, and helping others, I began to believe there was more to my life than my eating disorder and destructive behaviours. Not only did Heather and others at Norwich YFC give me this emotional support, they also gave me practical support. We would work out meal plans together, work out plans for getting me to college regularly and recognise the things that were negative in my life so I felt empowered to make a change. I noticed some books in the office called 'Cut' and 'Starved' by Nancy Alcorn - books about how to overcome eating disorders and self-harm. I worked through these with Heather and ended up staying in a residential home started by Nancy in America called Mercy. During my stay, staff at Norwich YFC and the friends I made at gospel choir wrote to me with letters of encouragement.

Since graduating from Mercy I have started working for another Youth for Christ centre in Norfolk (Integrate YFC) and encouraging young people in the area just as I was encouraged by Norwich Youth for Christ. I can honestly say that if I didn't have the support and help from NYFC I wouldn't be where I am today. Thank you!

Naomi Tate (née Ash-Lameer)

Naomi Tuma

What you have to understand is that as a teenager I didn't know that God lived in Norfolk!

I had just turned 16 and was studying for my Scottish Highers, I was pretty unhappy, bored and knew that staying at school would mean getting into drinking and drug taking. I had been praying about what to do and I said to God "I will go wherever". My youth leader was talking about gap years and had a pile of leaflets from different organisations, my decision was simple; who offered the most training and was the cheapest: Youth for Christ.

I was placed with Wymondham Baptist Church and I was part of a team of 16 students! I had a skinhead and a long fringe, so I looked a little bit punk! I was freaked out by how flat Norfolk is, and people didn't understand me because of my Scottish accent. Everybody had to ask me to slow down and to say everything twice.

My mentor was Helen Roberts and she was a really significant part of my journey. She even taught me how to hug! I was grumpy, unhappy and very sarcastic, - I didn't do hugging. Helen would say "Naomi I'm going to give you a hug, stand still. Naomi, you need to hug me back!" She encouraged me to engage with God even when I didn't feel like it. She taught me to persevere and keep going with it.

It was a really tricky year for me emotionally and spiritually. I had got to a point where I had said to God "If you're real then show me." Isaiah 54 popped into my head. I looked it up and it describes a woman who has had a really difficult youth and has felt abandoned by God, but He promises to restore her. I read it and thought "This describes my life!" I felt that God was saying 'I haven't abandoned you and I have a future for you'. I rang Helen and asked 'Does God normally speak to people like this'?! After that I decided to get baptised at the sea in Lowestoft with YFC. I had already planned to stay in Norfolk but wasn't sure how. The very next day I got an offer from UEA for a place. It felt like a confirmation I was on the right path.

During university I continued to be involved with NYFC at least once a week and helped with lots of things including Fridays, Living Water, Soul Survivor trips and I even helped write their first Child Protection policy! All of this gave me the skills to get a job as a sessional youthworker, and I've been working in youth and community work for the last 25 years.

While at UEA I also met a young man called Mark Tuma who was a worship leader for the Christian Union. NYFC needed some equipment for an event and I convinced Mark to lend them his guitar amp. He came to see the event, heard Ian speak, and signed up for a gap year... the rest is Mark's story!

It's hard to put into words how YFC has helped me. It wasn't about one incident but is more that without God working through YFC, the trajectory of my life would be entirely different.

Because of YFC, God was able to move me to a place I had never heard of before (I had to look Norwich up on a map to find out where it was) and discover "Ah! I have a Norfolk soul!". But also, the practice of Youth for Christ's theology is crucial to how I understand faith now.

Rather than getting bogged down in the details or arguments, they concentrate on the core bits that everyone agrees with and focus on the mission. They taught me, and continue to tell young people: God loves you, He's interested in your life and He has a plan for you. Now get on and be a part of that plan and we will support you.

Naomi Tuma

Neville Willerton

From 1993-1996, as an NYFC youth worker, I used to be based at Norwich Prison as part of the chaplaincy team mainly working with the young offenders. I took services, midweek Alpha course groups and supported the young offenders, many who were struggling with a lack of hope and loneliness.

I remember one service I organised when I brought a band into the prison to take an Easter service. The band brought all their equipment into the chapel including drums, guitars and speakers, the only problem was when of the band members accidently left his van keys in the van and shut the door – locked! I knew exactly what to do, I went down the landing and spoke to one of the inmates and gave him a letter opener – he had the van door open in two seconds flat.

I had the privilege of leading one young man to Christ in his cell. I spent time supporting him in his new faith and praying and studying the Bible together. I remember coming back to the prison after some annual leave and walking down the landing and seeing him running towards me. He told me that he has been sharing his faith to his friends in the prison and then told me 'See, it is not only you who can do it'. A quote from a letter I still have from one of the inmates who is called Martin. 'I am in Norwich prison but should be out soon. I am 18 years old and have one child and a very good girlfriend who has been very supportive since I have been away. I was not a Christian before I came inside and I had just given up on life altogether. But one day I turned my life to God and ever since that day my life has changed dramatically. I haven't been thinking of suicide or anything bad. I'm glad that Jesus is with me through the good times and the bad... My favourite Psalm is 51 – it means a lot to me when I sit here in my cell and get depressed. I turn to my Bible and read a few pages each night and learn a new thing about God each day'.

In 1996 I took a team of young people on mission from Norwich YFC to Poland Youth for Christ. We took over a financial gift from us to Poland YFC. We did lots of street evangelism in a town called Wroclaw by using fire juggling, drama and escapology. We even went into one of the prisons in Poland and took a service in the chapel. Many of the young people that we took over to Poland grew in confidence in their faith.

I remember praying with one man in the prison who was coping with lots of guilt from what he had done. We together asked for the Holy Spirit to come and release him from his pain and set him free. He fell down in the Spirit and was weeping uncontrollably - God was clearly at work in him. I remember hoping that the prison staff wouldn't walk in as I would have some serious explaining to do! After a few minutes he came round and I asked him what had God done – his reply was that he knew God's forgiveness! I will never forget that moment.

One funny story entailed one of the Operation Gideon year groups that we had in Norwich Youth for Christ. Two mischievous young Operation Gideon lads decided to strap a small plastic bottle full of milk to the back of one of our filing cabinets. After a few weeks of dreadful smells coming from our office we were convinced there was an animal dead under the floorboards. Then the bottle dropped from behind the filing cabinet and out seeped a congealed, foul smelling gunk from the bottle – we knew it was the two lads from Operation Gideon. However we got our own back on them – but that is another story…

Neville Willerton

Nick Blanch

Assemblies are usually a dull affair, especially for a teenage boy, but I always remember Simon Kirby and others from Norwich Youth for Christ visiting Hellesdon High School. Their energy and passion were always visible and brightened up the usual morning gathering.

I was at a church camp with Meadow Way Chapel, when I first said yes to Jesus. We were not a church going family and so I was the first in my family to do this (a lot has changed since then but that's another story!). However, as I reflect back on those NYFC assemblies, I feel sure that there was a healthy dose of seed planting going on.

Norwich Youth for Christ has often been in the background of my life, popping up time and again to encourage, challenge and inspire me. As a teenager, discovering the adventure of a life walking with Jesus, I was always hungry to learn and grow. When a little event called Living Waters started at the Norfolk Showground, my youth workers encouraged me to get along and I didn't hesitate.

This Christian weekend which gathered thousands together in expressive worship and brilliant teaching had Norwich Youth for Christ heading up the youthwork. I was introduced to a much bigger kingdom of followers than I had realised existed and I loved the opportunity to meet other teenagers from different churches

(It's also where I met the lovely Rebecca Fleetcroft who became my wife, but that is also another story!!).

I began to see NYFC operating more and more. I was always struck by how creative they were, taking risks and doing things that were contemporary for young people with the intentional aim of drawing them to Jesus. I dipped in and out and was able to take part in some of NYFC's drama productions which inspired me to try more of this in my own church.

I now have the privilege of working as Director and in my short time here, we've run a musical, made a series of films for our YouTube channel and launched a mobile recording studio. The tradition of using creativity to share the gospel is still alive and well! I think NYFC inspired me as a young person and it's amazing to input back into that, telling young people about Jesus in a relevant and modern way and hopefully inspiring the next generation to do the same!

Nick Blanch

Paul Gowing

I started attending NYFC in the 1980. Where most churches were still using hymn books, NYFC had a band and used overheads. My daughter hasn't a clue what these are! In 1984 (I think I've got the dates right), they ran the mission 'Down to Earth' where they encouraged people to use their skills\talents in everything from leading the worship to setting up the venue. The event ran every night for t weeks and introduced the churches into new forms of worship and many people were 'Saved' during these events.

The main thing about NYFC is that they allowed people to find out what their gifts were, by letting them to have a go and make mistakes. The churches at that time were reluctant (apart from a few) to allow the young people to do anything but sit in a pew.

From there as I grew older I aided the technical side of NYFC and worked on the amplification and lighting and under Ian did many musicals from 'The Gift' to 'The Blood of the Lamb'. Again, the main theme was to get young Christians involved in all aspects, from praying to setting up and clearing away the venues to leading groups\dance\drama and worship. It's this aspect that I hope NYFC continues, letting people find out what their gifts are and aiding them to grow and use them.

Then, of course, there was running the nightclub on a Sunday evening, the summer camps and Living Waters. NYFC was then at the forefront of doing things which were not out of the church manual, and which upset a lot of churches - I hope you continue with this tradition!

Paul Gowing

Pete Skivington

As a teenager growing up in Norfolk in the 1990's there were a few dates worth putting on the calendar - upcoming Norwich City fixtures (including top 3 Prem finish and UEFA cup run!), the latest Britpop bands to be performing at UEA and the Waterfront and of course the next NYFC Fridays event! These were my first experience of Norwich Youth for Christ. It was great to join with others from across the county to worship God and to be part of something bigger, connecting with those from other youth groups. Alongside that was the Sunday night youth events at Ikon which I and several mates used to attend.

Whilst in 6th form college I opted to do a work experience placement with NYFC. They were short on office space so I got to borrow the chair of the then Director, Ian Savory who was on sabbatical at the time. Now we share the pastor's office at Lighthouse Community Church in Sheringham - small world!

I've got many happy connections with YFC over the years, but for this article I'm focusing on Reality 06. It was a fantastic event bringing together Christians from across the city in praise and outreach. We gathered in the morning for teaching and worship at Princes Street United Reformed church. Then with the chorus "fill us up and send us out" ringing in our ears we were commissioned to go and be good news in local communities across the city, whatever that might look like in a variety of projects tailored by churches to meet local needs. I was living in Mile Cross at the time, and having recently worked for Christians in Sport I was asked to oversee a sports project engaging local children. I had a great team of enthusiastic volunteers and we spent the afternoons that week in glorious sunshine playing football, basketball, volleyball, unihoc and many more sports with some fantastic young people. Each day one of the team would share a bit about why they were a Christian and the difference Jesus made in their lives. The fact the temperatures were tropical meant we had lots of drinks breaks which was a great opportunity to chat with the kids about what had been said and for them to ask questions. We saw several youngsters followed up, growing in faith and connecting in with ongoing church youthwork in the area.

Some of the fruit from Reality was seen when the national mission initiative Hope 08 was launched; the churches in Mile Cross/Catton Grove had already formed strong links and partnered together in three more days of worship and outreach to the local community, including sport, gardening, arts and drama, culminating in a celebration BBQ with hundreds attending.

Rev Peter Skivington

Youth and Children's Pastor

Lighthouse Community Church

Phil Timson

Back in January 2012, I was invited to the Youth for Christ conference to share about HOPE and in particular my own role within the youth arm; HOPE Revolution and our 'Mission Academy' programme which seeks to empower young people to share their faith amongst their peers. Throughout the week I was casting vision and meeting with youth workers to get as many YFC centre's signed up to use Mission Academy. Norwich Youth for Christ had an immediate energy and drive for the project, catching the vision and getting the project going in Norwich later that year. They have since been one of the longest running Mission Academy projects, recognising its long-term value and sharing our heart to see young people equipped and empowered to share their faith.

In 2015 I was privileged to be invited to their youth worship service 'Encounter' as a part of our 'Step Out Tour', which challenged young people to commit their lives to Jesus and to continually step out for the gospel. We ended the evening with a response time which saw God move powerfully with a tangible sense of His presence. Praise God, twenty young people made decisions to follow Jesus that night with at least another sixty committed to step out more and take ongoing risks in their daily pursuit of Jesus. I believe this event highlights something of the journey and culture that NYFC raises. Some events can simply feel dry, but here there was a natural excitement, with a heightened spiritual atmosphere and readiness to pursue Jesus amongst young people, that I believe enabled God to move in a powerful way. Young people were then encouraged by NYFC to sign up for the next Mission Academy and we had over thirty put their names down to commit to this process. I loved NYFC's intentionality, to give an immediate tangible opportunity for young people to grab hold of. It's another example of how NYFC build strategy and support to see long term growth rather than just running a one-off event. Great work all!

More recently, NYFC have been instrumental in helping us connect and work in partnership with more youth workers across the Norfolk region, gathering people from across churches and organisations to be a catalyst for unity and for the pioneering of new things that will come as a result.

Over many years, NYFC have been a fantastic advocate for HOPE, championing the cause of peer-to-peer evangelism, engaging with the evangelistic tours, delivering the Mission Academies, and gathering leaders together to dream for the Kingdom. We love you all and have loved the privilege of working in partnership together and we look forward to all that is yet to come through your ongoing faithfulness and obedience! Bring it on!

Phil Timson

HOPE Youth Director

Rachel Varley

I have so many happy memories of spending time with the NYFC team and attending events throughout my teenage years. Growing up in a Christian family, I was encouraged to get stuck into church related things and after seeing both of my siblings really enjoying events like Fridays, I couldn't wait until I was old enough to go along.

I can remember the first time my mum said I was old enough to go to Fridays – such excitement! I remember arriving and instantly being invited to join the welcome team. From then on I felt very welcomed and it wasn't long before friends were coming along too. Fridays was an amazing place to gather with others of the same age, exploring what faith means and how to dig deeper into God. It was a lot of fun!

NYFC introduced me to the idea of 'social action' and showing God's love in practical ways through projects such as Reality and Hope on the Streets. We picked up litter, beautified gardens and ran holiday clubs – all for the sake of showing God's love to our neighbours. We got to spend time and serve in different communities which opened my eyes to see things from a new perspective.

One key project that NYFC ran for a few years was 'The Forum', an online social networking site (before the days of Facebook!). It was a space for us to connect with other young people and discuss the big and small issues of life. It was a great place to learn others' opinions on different topics and to wrestle with our own ideas of who God is. I am so grateful that we had that safe space.

NYFC provided opportunities to not only connect with other Christians, but to invite my non-Christian friends along to as well. Occasions like the Christmas balls for example. We had SO much fun and it was a great way to cross the divide between Christian and non-Christian friends.

There are so many more things I could talk about that NYFC provided during those years... girls' weekends away, Gospel Choir, Restore Café, Youth Alpha, Soul Survivor trips, support at our school Christian Union, etc.

The NYFC team were a huge support to me when I found out my A Level results (whilst at Soul Survivor with them!). I didn't get the grades I needed to go to university that year which was a huge shock. However, during my unplanned gap year, the team were a constant source of encouragement and fun.

I am so grateful to all the staff, volunteers and trustees who have caught the vision of seeing the lives of young people changed by God and committed to partnering with God in that in Norwich. God has, not only given me a firm foundation for my life, but impacted the lives of my friends and family too.

Rachel Varley

Rob Wilson

I first got involved with NYFC by going along to a Rock Solid group run by Paul Roast and other volunteers. It was a really great group where we met together, chatted and played silly games. I really enjoyed this as it let me meet with other Christians my age and grapple with what Christianity meant to me. This mostly happened with chatting to Paul about different concepts like predestination and spiritual gifts which I found fascinating.

From Rock Solid, I joined the NYFC Gospel Choir which is something I never thought I would do but I really enjoyed the sense of community it had (it was family). Choir for me wasn't about the performances but about the rehearsals and how they gave me a time to laugh with friends at the back of choir and sing some great worship songs that gave me life for the rest of the week.

I remember the lads' group which was great to do life with fellow guys and chat about Jesus and how we can best follow Jesus - interspersed with lots of food, movies and general chat. I remember the first breakfast which was planned early in the morning at a shocking 9am (how they expect teenage boys to be awake at that time I have no idea). I turned up slightly late yet still before everyone else and decided to help Pete Tyson who asked me to finish making the coffee. I proceeded to spectacularly fail to use a cafetière properly and then managed to tip it over, pouring coffee all over the floor in my extremely tired state. This just makes me think how amazing the youth workers at NYFC are - that they can survive and help us when we continually spill coffee everywhere and show up late! Yet, they still manage to show God's love to us.

It was this, and a bit of prayer with God, which made me to want to spend a year out with NYFC because they are the ones who really do follow the commandments of loving your neighbour as yourself. It was one of the best decisions of my life and I learnt so much about living a missional life and youth work.

The real crux of what NYFC is to me is family and journeying together. They are great at meeting me and others where we are at and push us a bit further into exploring faith and God. I wouldn't be where I am in my faith without NYFC.

Rob Wilson

Roy Crowne

Norwich Youth for Christ has been an amazing and effective ministry. My first encounter with NYFC was when I was an evangelist with British Youth for Christ, in a garage as part of the team that were running a mission called 'Down to Earth'. It was my privilege to work alongside Norwich YFC, Eric Delve and J John in this mission where the churches in Norwich had taken over an old derelict garage on a corner in the city centre and had transformed it into a venue for a gospel presentation. It was so fruitful that we had to continue for an extra week; the response of young people particularly to the gospel, was phenomenal.

I have some really fond memories of the school lessons that were taken, assemblies and the overall impact of that mission and I am convinced that there are lives and people that are part of the church who came to Christ as a result of this time.

Norwich YFC have had some of the best Directors, many of whom are still in the area. Some were real close friends, Geoff Lawton, Grantley Watkins and Ian Savory just to name a few.

It was a real privilege to join with Norwich YFC during my time as National Director with BYFC. Their innovation continued to move into the nightclub world where, through the leadership, they had secured chaplaincy in two of the nightclubs in Norwich and to work alongside the bishop to see the night time economy embracing NYFC's strategy in building chaplaincy into a nightclub. It was so successful that they could met real needs, where people were expressing amazing unconditional love as well as practical service and seeing some of those people realise the impact of NYFC at some of their most emotional and vulnerable moments with the physical challenges of alcohol, NYFC was there to serve.

It was great to see Norwich taking a lead on this and also to see it recognised by the chain of nightclubs that they were working with, and wanted to encourage this across the country. This enabled them to hold a worship experience in the same club on a Monday night when the nightclub wasn't open. It is this kind of innovation that Norwich YFC has continued to do with musicals, choirs and dessert evenings for supporters, staying true to the gospel.

It's great that Norwich YFC has continued to innovate but also continued in its core and we as HOPE are thrilled to be partnering with them on Mission Academy, a discipleship and evangelism programme. It's great to know that in the city of Norwich NYFC continues to serve the young people with the Gospel.

Innovation has always been a key element of all that they do. Well done NYFC. May you innovate, create and continue to see the gospel change lives.

Roy Crowne

HOPE Executive Director

Ruth MacCormack

I helped at NYFC from approximately 1993 for about ten years. I was mainly involved in prayer ministries at Fridays and Living Water but I also helped "police" at Ritzy's with the nightclub ministry. I also sang in the various choirs and really was happy to help with anything. My whole involvement was a privilege. I loved working with the various teams and the young people were a joy....(Nick Blanch was one of them!). Both my daughters were also very much involved with one of them doing a part time GAP year....during this time they both made commitments to Jesus.

I also financially supported some of the youth workers during this time and today still give a little on a monthly basis.

I believe Norwich has benefited greatly from the input of YFC and its various directors.

Ruth MacCormack

Sally McNeish

I arrived in Norwich YFC as a 17 year old freshly released into the adult world on a scheme called Operation Gideon. Having decided God definitely wanted to shake me out of my sheltered upbringing, I underwent the training course in Birmingham, braced myself for tough urban realities of inner city youthwork and found myself in rural Norfolk.

Thank God I did! In a year riddled with instability and change both within and around me, NYFC provided a safe haven.

Ian Savory was a calm, wise captain with a wicked twinkle in his eye, while Margie Bone was like a mother to me that year through real turbulence as I learned just how much growing up I still had to do. Their influence was one of the things I look back on as formative in my life and faith; their kindness, compassion, cool common sense and naughty streak of fun were a real anchor and inspiration.

Tracey's nightclub chaplaincy work was also an inspiring world to discover (once I was old enough!); I loved the creativity with which she could be herself and make a big difference to others too, bringing compassion very naturally wherever she went.

Very sadly we lost Jenny, our local team coordinator, during the course of that year. Her gentle thoughtfulness had helped us all to feel welcome and her death was a huge shock to everyone. Ian and

Margie were again very important in helping us through what must have been a deep sorrow for themselves.

I haven't been back to visit NYFC but I have stayed in touch with Margie over the years. Looking back in my diary from that time I discovered frequent mention of "Prayer and toast". I can't think of a better summary of the team than this phrase provides; a great marriage of faith and warm practicality. Thank you NYFC!

Sally McNeish (née Anderson)

Sarah Weller

My first contact with NYFC was in the days when Ian Savory was in charge, with Helen, Tim, Margie and Tracey supporting him. It is hard to narrow down to any one particular event how NYFC has helped and encouraged me as there were so many.

Going along to the monthly Friday night events in Norwich was a real encouragement as I and my friends grew up in one of the village churches where there weren't many other young people. It was also good because I got to realise that hot Christian guys didn't just go to Spring Harvest!

I was part of the drama team led by Helen that performed a play she had written about how Christianity had come to Norwich at one of the events celebrating the work of NYFC, (possibly their 16th Birthday celebrations?). It was great being part of that and as I got older and went to College I began to attend some of the courses that NYFC ran, and helped on teams at Living Water which had just started up.

I can honestly say that NYFC has played a significant part in my Christian journey. The team gave me confidence to share my faith and to use the gifts God had given me. I remember sitting down with Ian Savory on one occasion and talking about what God might want to do with my life and how he just encouraged me to focus on Him. The team at NYFC believed in me and I will never forget that.

Sarah Weller

Simon Faulks

Every journey has its key points, whether it's a short walk to the local shop and a simple 'turn left at the end of the road', or the more major journeys that involve planned stops. Our life journeys are no different; we have those small moments (a slight change in things) and then there are the big changes, the 'stop and swap driver' type changes. Norwich Youth for Christ was one of the latter type of key points in my journey.

I came to NYFC later in life than many, being in my late teens. Having grown up in the village of Mulbarton in a Christian home, I had been aware of them for many years but not involved. In the early 1990's I had gone back to education at City College during a period of unemployment and there, through the CU, I got to know some others who went along to Fridays, an NYFC monthly youth worship event. I was nearer the age of the OP GID gap year students than many of the others, but seeing these like-minded people dedicated to God was an encouragement. Although there were other young Christians in the village, they were mostly two or three years from my age.

There were many things that happened: residential and all night events, being on the team running one of the cafés at Soul Survivor and later involvement in the youth side of the Living Waters event on the Norfolk showground. But I have to say it is not really the specifics that have stuck with me through the years. The team at NYFC placed value on everyone who was involved at whatever level, they gave me opportunities to get involved, to have a go.

Either directly or indirectly it was through NYFC that I went into a school to talk to a CU for the first time, and I had a chance to be involved in planning and producing material for Fridays. Unlike my schooling which had left me feeling incapable, NYFC helped me to feel empowered by God.

What might have seemed like one of those smaller key points at the time, when I look back, I see that, along with others, my involvement with NYFC was a significant point in my life and my journey with God. By the mid 90's I was off to Bible College, by the late 90's I was a church-based youth worker, after ten years in youth ministry I went back to Bible College again and I am now a Church of England Rector of five rural parishes. I am privileged to see and be part of God equipping and encouraging people of all ages and from all backgrounds, but specifically in the rural church as they discover some of those key changes in the life journey that God has for them.

Rev Simon Faulks

Parishes of Newton Longville, Mursley, Little Horwood, Swanbourne and Drayton Parslow

Simon Kirby

What memories! There were obviously the dressing up occasions at Fridays - Ian Savory particularly enjoyed dressing up. The two events I remember were when the team dressed up as nuns and did a dance to a Sister Act number as the guest speaker had written a fairly bad review about Sister Act in Christianity magazine the previous week. He didn't find it that funny!

On another occasion we also dressed in boots and tutus to perform a liturgical dance. I remember kidnapping and dumping some of our year out students on the edge of Norwich to walk home after they had deliberately hidden some milk around the NYFC office to go off and stink the place out!

I remember some epic residentials including the SOGITS weekends (Serious on God Intensive Training).

More seriously Sue and I met through YFC when we were sent to Norwich together, me to work in Oak Grove with the Op Gid team and Sue as a second year trainee centre worker. We had an association with NYFC for the best part of the next ten years as Sue stayed on as a staff worker and I headed to Bible College before we got married in 1991 at a wedding with lots of YFC friends. We returned to Norwich in 1992 when I started as the schools worker and had five very happy years with NYFC during which time both of the boys were born. We moved to London in 1997 where I took up the post of youth worker in a fairly large Anglican church and started the journey to ordination. Now, as we minister in Oxfordshire, we're so grateful for the values we learnt, the friendships we made and the fun we had as part of NYFC and I'm delighted that we're investing heavily into youth and children's work here at St Mary's, Cogges.

Rev Simon Kirby

Vicar of Cogges, North Leigh & South Leigh

Simon Oliver

I had the privilege of being part of NYFC from 1996-1999, first in Stoke Holy Cross (with the notorious-but-actually–quite-lovely Stoke Boys) as part of a national scheme called Operation Gideon, after which I stayed on to form the Herbert Drama Company which toured schools, churches and festivals and was based at Oak Grove Chapel.

My time coincided with the benevolent dictatorship of Ian Savory's goatee. There are too many other people to name personally, but special mention should go to our two Herbert teams which included the talents of Jonny Hate, Matt Hunt, Hazel and Zoe Magrath, Martin Eden Fallon, Tim Strudwick, Nathan Philips, Louise Morgan and Gary Daniel. Amazing people that I've sadly managed to almost entirely lose touch with.

From sublimely choreographed dance routines to shambolic strip teases, from slapstick comedy to poignant monologues, from rapturous applause and lives seemingly touched to being heckled by teachers in schools and banned from certain churches, from drag racing to dressing in drag, from smoking in church to being soaked at Living Waters, from being kidnapped (twice) to making an entire primary school cry with a Christmas presentation, they were rich, full and formative years.

In all of this, I am incredibly grateful to have been loved, supported, and set free to take risks for the sake of the Gospel and the young people and churches we sought to minister with. In the years since I have attempted to carry something of this inclusive, far-reaching, risk-taking ethos with me into my various endeavours since in both ministry and the arts, and now as an ordained pioneer Methodist Minister near Cambridge.

Rev Simon Oliver

Methodist Pioneer Minister in Cottenham

Sophie Gathercole

NYFC saved my life.

I first came into contact with NYFC when I was 13. We had a new youth worker at our church and initially I was anxious and dubious about yet another new face in the church but I got to know him and it was the beginning of a relationship that, down the line, ultimately saved my life.

I began to experience some mental health problems at 13 and like most teenagers, didn't know what to do with myself. My problems got worse and worse and I felt myself losing all control but I didn't have anyone that I could talk to. As I became more involved with Church and the youth group it ran, I got to know Paul and began to talk to him. Not openly at first but it started the relationship. After a few months, Paul always used to ask how I was and I always used to reply 'I'm fine' when really I was swimming in a veritable pool of depression, anxiety and self-harm issues. Anyway, I began to trust Paul and started to confide in him. He always gave me time and space to talk about my issues and while having no professional training, you wouldn't believe the helpful, counselling and spiritual advice that he used to come back with. Paul was always there to help through my problems and even just a listening ear was something I really treasured.

Paul used to meet up with me once a week to check up and see how things were going. It was important to me to be able to vent and talking about stuff stopped me bottling it up which meant that I didn't get to the point where I really couldn't cope anymore. I will always be thankful to Paul for being that listening ear and offering such good advice, which stopped me planning on killing myself and that is something really special. I feel I should say more about how much Paul and NYFC helped me but really the crux of the matter is, is that if it hadn't been for them, I would not be alive today. It was the sheer caring nature of the staff that made the difference in my life and I am eternally grateful.

After a while I began to volunteer for them and helped with a number of things from lunch clubs in schools, assemblies, camps, projects such as 'Who Cares?' and youth work at my local church. I wanted to help and be a part of that mission, changing people's lives and helping them experience what faith is and how it can help, and how NYFC is changing the stereotype and making a difference in the lives of young people in Norwich. It was really fun volunteering with NYFC. We had a laugh with everything we did and it made a difference to me to be making a difference to others. Paul and Nick were great mentors and taught me a lot about youth work and how to engage with young people, I really enjoyed learning and putting what I'd learnt into action. It was soon after I started volunteering that I became the mentor for other young people, chatting with them and listening in the same way Paul had for me. It broke my heart to hear what others had gone through but the fact that I was a part of NYFC and had the tools I needed to help them deal with it was really special.

NYFC have left a lasting legacy with me and I am really passionate about their work. I hope to one day get back to volunteering and helping alongside NYFC. NYFC saved me from a life of misery and despair and ultimately saved me from suicide purely through their ability to listen and give advice and I will never be able to pay them back for that. It's nice to keep in contact and I am very proud to have been a part of NYFC's work.

Sophie Gathercole

Steph Richardson

For many years we had provided youth work in our local area in Diss on a voluntary basis. We had formed some good links with Mid Norfolk Youth for Christ (in Dereham) and they gave us the initial idea to form a centre. When we decided to take this forward and start the process they put us in touch with Mark Tuma, the then Director of Norwich Youth for Christ. Myself and my husband Jonathan had some previous experience with NYFC as we used to take young people to Fridays (see his own story about his experiences!), so it was another positive YFC link.

Although we felt it was the right thing to do, none of us was a trained youth worker so it felt quite daunting to suddenly be more official. It is one thing to gather volunteers to do some youth work on a mutual basis but quite another to become an organisation heading it up! Mark was brilliant as we started the process. He came to all our trustees' meetings when we first started and talked through all the different things we needed to do to become a charity and helped us through the process to become Integrate Youth for Christ

Mark also coached me for the first year, helping to understand my role as Director and encouraging me to keep going. This was very helpful especially when I didn't feel like a Director! It helped me work out the vision for the centre as well as the practicalities of generating financial support. He would push me to get out of my comfort zone and do things that I didn't think I would be able to do. For example, the thought of visiting churches and telling them what we do was quite daunting as I wasn't used to public speaking but Mark's encouragement gave me the confidence I needed to let people know about the work we were doing!

For me, stepping into that role was a big leap and without Mark to guide us we would have really struggled so he was a key aspect in our journey, building confidence for our centre and moving me into that role. I'm thankful for the release of Mark's time from NYFC for this.

Mark was therefore the link person who introduced us to the wider YFC family and made us feel part of it. We have regular East Anglian meetings with other local Directors and at that time Mark was organising those meetings. I really value these times together, having other people in similar positions who you can talk to and having that mutual support together.

The process took about a year for us to become a YFC centre. We have now been going for just over eight years and the amount we are doing now is way more than we could ever have envisaged or imagined when we started.

When we first launched we were all voluntary but now we have three part time paid staff and a large number of volunteers. We started with one youth cafe and two lunchtime clubs. Now we run four youth cafes, four lunchtime clubs in high schools, sixth form mentoring, discipling groups, residentials, prayer spaces in schools, schools missions and have developed the work to include the Thetford area in the last eighteen months.

We would never imagined how far we would come! We're still on a shoestring and limited budget but somehow we still manage!

Steph Richardson

Director

Integrate Youth for Christ

Steve Biltawi

On 9th October 1993, I made the long journey to Norwich to start my Operation Gideon year with Youth for Christ. It was a fantastic, crazy, fun, challenging year that gave me masses of opportunity to have a go, try again and discover my gifts.

Coming from Barnsley, my accent was strong which meant that I couldn't understand Norwich people and they couldn't understand me. When I helped Simon Kirby in schools work, he would nurse me in my speech, telling me to slow down and giving me elocution lessons so that people could understand. He stitched me up a few times though, once asking me in an assembly who my favourite football team was. Of course, I said Manchester United and the place erupted with boos!

I am not a morning person, so when I discovered that every Friday morning at 7am we had something called 'prayer and toast' on our timetable, I could have cried. But there was a real sense of encountering God's presence at these meetings and although I was tired, it became a brilliant platform for the rest of the day, especially if you were going into Fridays which meant a long day and evening. The value on prayer and mission together was really key to NYFC's success. It was like a honey pot; young people would orbit around these events, because of the prayer work.

The nightclub work hadn't been going for long when I was there but I loved hearing the vision behind it, how Ian felt challenged by

God about what the church was doing fort those people who needed help after a drunken night out. When I first went into Ritzy's nightclub, it was with a bit of trepidation, but Tracey Hyslop was working there as an NYFC chaplain and she introduced us to the different staff members and some of the clients. I had a long conversation with a clubber called Ziggy. There was such a desperation in him but that night I was able to share the gospel with him. In the nightclub work, it was being light in a dark place. The message wasn't watered down, just carried in a different way.

The Operation Gideon's based in Norwich that year was made up of eight people (two teams of four). Helen (Windsor/Roberts) really looked after us and the various issues that naturally came up in teams. All teams hit challenges and when the honeymoon phase was over there was a moment where we were struggling. Outwardly we were professional but inwardly we were a bit tired of each other. Ian called us into the office one afternoon to hear our complaints and whinges. He listened to us without saying anything. Finally he asked us to take our socks and shoes off and he walked out. We all thought 'why are we taking our socks and shoes off?!'. He came back with some warm soapy water. I asked him what he was doing and he told us "I'm going to wash your feet". And he did. He washed our feet and prayed for us. It showed how silly our complaints were, we all apologised and that night we went out to the cinema together. Before that meeting, I couldn't see how we could get things resolved, but in the end it came quickly because Ian showed us what servant leadership looked like.

Some of the best conversations I had with Ian were after events when he was brushing up afterwards, He was always the last one out and Sue was always washing up, laughing and spraying suds at everybody. One thing that has stuck with me is when Ian told me "Whatever you do, make it as hard as possible for someone to become a follower of Jesus". I've seen every other strategy to make it easy for someone to follow Jesus. But he taught me that following Jesus is a lifelong commitment, it's about taking your cross up, dying to yourself and living in the power of his resurrection.

I left Norwich July '94 for Warrington where I completed another two years on Operation Gideon) I kept in contact for a number of years afterwards, often coming back to volunteer at the summer events. In 1996 I became a staff worker at Warrington YFC and then from 2000 -2007 I served as Director. Norwich was a brilliant foundational year.

One last memory - Simon Kirby took me for my first Balti curry at the Passage to India. It was amazing! Thank you, Jesus, for Simon Kirby and the Passage to India!

Steve Biltawi

Stuart Riddington

My dad had been a trustee for Norwich Youth for Christ and so from the age of 13 onwards I got involved in loads of their projects. Even at a young age, I was given lots of opportunities to get involved including helping at Living Waters, heading up Supernova with Tracey Hyslop and being able to speak at Fridays. It was a huge risk for someone so young.

One of my favourite stories is when we did some street evangelism outside C & A at the Haymarket. There was a small team of us and we would do a little routine which involved two of us standing opposite each other at either end of the quad. We would shout to each other and then run across the area to reach the other person but then miss on purpose. We would do this a few times to draw attention and gain a crowd for someone to then do a small talk. But on one occasion, we were approached by two police officers who wanted to arrest us for breach of the peace! Thankfully, someone on the team was married to a woman, whose father was the Deputy Police Constable for Norfolk. When he made mention of this the police officers suddenly backed off and left with a quick telling off to us to calm things down and not make so much noise. The irony being, we certainly had the desired effect of drawing a crowd as it swelled to about 200 people who were watching this unfold! We couldn't have had a better show for them!

I still have vivid memories of Supernova. This was a project where we took over a nightclub for the Sunday evening and made it available to under 16's. It was pretty controversial at the time and many churches didn't agree with it. But it was massively attended and we often had to turn young people away. The team first had to clean the whole club which was usually pretty disgusting from the night before. We once had a blocked toilet and on closer inspection we found a t-shirt stuffed down there and wrapped inside was a lovely poo!

When we opened, we always started with half an hour of dance worship - dance music but with Christian lyrics and artists. It was really cutting edge youth work and looking back it makes you realise the number of seeds that were sown into thousands of young people's lives.

Throughout this time, Ian mentored me and helped me to think. He encouraged me to see that Christianity was bigger, that it was relevant and real. With his encouragement, as a 16 year old, I did a year out with Oasis in Newcastle and then a year in Tanzania. Ian encouraged me to go to Moorlands and provided me with a reference.

Over the years I've been a pastor in Norwich, Cambridge, Bournemouth and the US! I've been able to work with some of the biggest names in the Christian world and for me, it all boils down to Ian taking the time and Youth for Christ investing in me at an early age. I just don't think I would be where I am today without the mentoring, opportunities and encouragement from Ian and others at Norwich Youth for Christ.

Stuart Riddington

Susanna Bornman

My teenage years were shaped by the impact Norwich Youth for Christ had on me. My Christian faith developed and was sustained and strengthened as a result of their influence. I believe the consistent witness and teaching of staff members at NYFC, as well as the friendships I built while I was involved in their ministry, influenced my whole outlook on life. God really worked through them to nurture my spiritual growth.

I first came into contact with the work of NYFC during the late '90's when a Christian friend from school invited me along to one of their monthly "Fridays" events. This was an opportunity to meet with other young Christians, to praise God in worship and receive teaching. After attending that first event, I never looked back, and became a regular attender of Fridays for many years to come! The teaching at Fridays spoke powerfully to me; helping me to understand how the truths of the Bible had direct relevance for my age group. The musical worship gave me an opportunity to draw closer to God and to freely express my thankfulness to Him.

As a teenager and young adult I was quite shy and lacking in self-confidence. However staff at NYFC encouraged me and believed in me, and they gave me opportunities to use my gifts. I soon became actively involved in various ways; for example writing scripts for dramas, and playing the flute as part of the Fridays worship band. As a result of this involvement I formed a number of really strong friendships. In particular I felt supported by other members of the Fridays worship band, as we had the opportunity to regularly meet together, worship God and pray together. I felt part of a community that was actively seeking to live for Christ and glorify him.

The friends I made through Youth for Christ were there to support me, pray with me and provide wise, Biblical council during some very difficult circumstances; including a time when my mum was critically ill, and after her death in 2004.

I am truly grateful to God for the way He impacted my life through Norwich Youth for Christ. Over many years I felt loved by Jesus through their work, and through the friendships I made there. This helped equip me to serve Him and love others, both at that time, and in the years since moving away from Norwich and continuing my Christian journey.

Susanna Bornman

Thea Smith

All I just want to say is 'thank you'.

Thank you for the people. Thank you for being an inspiring organisation that invests into others. Thank you for taking risks with young people. Thank you for giving me and others opportunities to have a go. Thank you because personal faith becomes a reality when you get to do stuff and step out.

As a teenager, living in a tiny little village outside of Norwich, although I had a good youth group in my local church, being able to join together with a large group of young people at Norwich Youth For Christ events was such a huge encouragement and I made some great friends going along to things like Fridays'

I remember Ian Savory used to say "You give your best away"; he helped to create a culture in Norwich YFC of equipping and releasing which is challenging and exciting for all involved and something all those involved in Christian Leadership could learn a lot from. There was always a constant practice of allowing young people to speak, serve and lead worship as well as other leadership opportunities. If it wasn't for that I don't know if so many would have gone on to be involved in ministry in later life (and stayed the distance).

At the age of 14, I had an incredible experience with a separate project called Street Life. Over my summer holidays I spent 2 weeks on mission, Modelled on Luke chapter 10 in the bible 'Jesus sends out the 72' we were dropped off in a location and then just had to trust in Jesus to look for opportunities to share the gospel, as well as where to stay and provision of food. It was my first real taste of evangelism and I loved it.

After that I got more involved with Waveney Youth for Christ and Norwich YFC. I went to as much as I could, including Fridays, the May Day event and Living Waters. I remember going to a residential weekend run by NYFC for those involved in running Christian Unions in their schools; the training was both practical and fun. Tracey Hyslop and Helen Roberts were involved and for some bizarre reason, at the meal time, they served me (and only me) ice cream with sausages!

As well as leading the Christian Union, I set up a prayer meeting at the school and even took assemblies. I remember my head teacher calling me to his office and asking me to pray for another student who he believed maybe involved in the occult! I think a lot of this stuff was happening because NYFC just kept inspiring you to take risks and have a go! I learnt that if you trust Jesus, it might be a bit wild and crazy at times, but it turns out ok in the end. You can trust him, really trust him.

In 2001 I moved up North to work for Warrington Youth for Christ as Senior Youth Worker. Ten years later I then started work at British Youth for Christ as part of the local ministries team, supporting and helping to set up local centres. Although I left East Anglia in 2001, Norwich has always held a special place in my heart and when my role included supporting YFC centres in the East I was delighted and I count it a real honour and privilege to support

Nick, the team and trustees as they continue their mission in Norwich of seeing young people's lives changed by Jesus.

So thank you, thank you Youth For Christ for taking young people and giving them a chance even if they don't have it all sorted.

Thank you, God, for Youth for Christ – for all it's done in the past and thank you that 'the best is yet to come'

Thea Smith (née Pitchers)

Local Ministries Development Manager

Youth for Christ

p.s. Eric and Margie Bone are legends - they still pray for me now!

Tim Yau

I worked with Norwich Youth for Christ from 1997 to 2002 as the Schools' Worker. When I arrived in the city I was fresh-faced from two years with the then National Youth for Christ's volunteer programme 'Operation Gideon'. Looking back I was overly idealistic and rather naive, but full of enthusiasm and belief that God was going to turn up on my watch and sort the world out.

As a career move, working for NYFC was imprudent as the salary was low and finances were shaky, but as a step-of-faith it was priceless, because I was stretched and formed as a disciple. In those days money was often tight and at the end of the month we regularly prayed and thanked God for His provision, even though we were often faced with an empty bank balance. For this reason we were very grateful for small things and treasured little treats, that today I sometimes take for granted.

I remember Gill, one of our key volunteers; her little treat was new clothes. She had managed to save up, find a bargain and bought herself a stylish jumper that she loved. That week we were running a music cafe in a marquee at the Soul Survivor Youth Festival down in Somerset. The place was buzzing with activity and playful laughter. Suddenly the cheerful atmosphere was punctuated with a shriek. Gill was aghast, she'd been cleaning and her new purchase was covered in bleach. The fading was already beginning to show. Gill's eyes began to fill with tears of frustration; we all knew what this little treat had meant to her.

One by one the team of volunteers began to gather up the little cash that they had and placed it in front of Gill. These were not rich people, they were mostly young people with little spare money, but they knew what it meant to their friend. What started out as frustrating accident turned into a festival of giving and by the end there was jubilant laughter and joyous tears all around that tent as Gill received more than a new jumper! The scripture that comes to mind is:

All the believers were one in heart and mind. No one claimed that any of their possessions was their own, but they shared everything they had. Acts 4:32

Moving to Norwich and being out-and-about wherever young people were was a time of great creativity, faith-building and laughter. However, being on the frontline with some of the most disaffected young people I've ever met eventually took its emotional toll on me. I could not save these young people, only God in in His timing could do that. On the way, I had some great experiences and saw some genuine change, but enthusiasm and confidence are not enough for the enormity of the task. God works to an eternal timescale and not our limited one, hence NYFC are still here twenty years on and still need to be here until God has finished what he started.

Rev Tim Yau

Pioneer Missioner

Norwich Diocese

Tracey Hyslop

During my years with Norwich Youth for Christ I had the privilege of serving God by developing the work we did in the nightclubs of the city. Through that work we shared the gospel but didn't always do it by preaching. Often it was our actions that spoke louder about the God we served, our faith in Him and our hope for salvation, than any of our words.

A very wise Christian lady once said that it was our job as God's servants to make space for every individual who didn't know him to be able to experience the grace of God in their lives. For me that was an aim I tried to fulfil through my work in the clubs and still do every day of my life now.

One story that really sticks to mind from those years involved a young gentleman we will call Tom. The pastoral advisor team in ikon was asked to come to the front door after one of the club's door supervisors noticed Tom staggering across the road, being helped by his friend but looking in very vulnerable state. We went out to investigate and very quickly identified that he needed help. He began to be sick and it was then we realised that the situation was perhaps even more serious than initially suspected as Tom was throwing up quite a lot of blood. Tom noticed the blood and got very frightened, asking is if we thought he was going to die. We told him we hoped not and got his permission to take him to the hospital.

Once at the hospital it was very clear how pale and poorly Tom was. Hospital staff responded almost immediately; rushed him round to one of the bays and hooked him up to some oxygen. We let the doctors do their work and then went round to see Tom. Tom told us that the doctors said he was very lucky; that if he hadn't come to the hospital he would have most likely have died as the alcohol he had consumed (he said - only about 3 bottles of beer) had had a very strong reaction to some medication he was on. The doctor said he wasn't out of danger yet but that they were hopeful.

We suggested someone perhaps needed to call his dad who we thought might be worried as he wasn't going home any time soon and may want to come to hospital given the severity of the situation. He agreed and gave one of us his dad's number. Tom was still very frightened and asked if we would stay with him until his dad got there. We said of course we would. His friend told us - out of Tom's earshot - that Tom and his dad had a very difficult relationship and he didn't believe his dad would actually come. His dad did come to the hospital but not but not for about six hours.

Tom never forgot how the team helped him that night. A couple of years later he came into the club with a young girl he had been dating for a while and introduced her to us as the team that saved his life. A couple of years after that we were asked to come to the front door. Tom was there with the same girl we had seen many times since and their small baby girl who they both insisted we met as they believed she would have never existed without our involvement that night years previously.

That story really reminds me again and again the impact one act of kindness done in God's name can have - it has the potential to outlast a lifetime, by even impacting future generations.

Tracey Hyslop

Wioletta Williams
YFC Poland

As soon as I started working with YFC Poland in 2001, I kept hearing about the wonderful NYFC team that had been our ministry partners for as long as we both existed. I heard about NYFC teams coming to Wroclaw and ministering to people in the ghetto-like area of the city that got completely flooded in 1997. I heard about NYFC's generosity in giving financially towards YFC Poland's outreach projects. And then a few years later, I did not just hear those good things, but I became the recipient of all the blessings coming from that partnership. First of all, I had the privilege to meet four different NYFC directors. Each encounter was an eye-opener. I was startled by the leaders' courage, faith and passion for youth. All the trips to Norwich inspired me to think bigger and braver in terms of what God might do among Polish youth.

Secondly, God blessed me with a role model of a totally God-dependent YFC director. Mark Tuma, the incredibly godly and humble man, became such a role model to me when I became YFC Poland's National Director. As the leader, I faced a tough time - shortage of staff and funds. Mark and his team were challenged in a similar way. Yet, it was them who taught me to believe in God's provision despite empty bank accounts. I will never forget the time when I said to Mark that we would understand if NYFC stopped supporting us to take care of their own needs (at that time we had only two supporters - NYFC and YFC Warrington). Mark's response was mind-blowing. He said that no matter how hard their financial situation might be, the support that went towards youth ministry in Poland was their tithing and obedience to God to share with their fellow believers whatever little they had. I will always be grateful to NYFC for that lesson on giving.

Thirdly, I am grateful that NYFC has responded to Jesus's calling to "go into the **whole** world and preach the Good News to everyone." In April 2011, Mark Tuma and Heather Land brought NYFC choir and within a week they managed to share the Gospel with a couple of hundred teenagers in two schools in Wroclaw as well as go into the streets of the city with the Gospel. Some teenagers that made friends with NYFC team members have been spiritually encouraged and today they themselves witness to their peers.

Finally, it is good to know that the NYFC and YFC Poland partnership has impacted young people on both sides. NYFC's support has allowed YFC Poland to minister to thousands of young people over a few decades. At the same time, I know that the English youth that came to work alongside us went back home changed spiritually too. So, we are forever grateful to God for our partnership with NYFC. May the Lord bless you richly!

Wioletta Williams

YFC Poland's ex-National Director, currently YFC Poland trustee

Afterword

I hope you've enjoyed our 40th Birthday book and felt encouraged by what God can do with ordinary people who have a heart for teenagers in Norwich to experience the transformational power of Jesus.

Would you like to be part of creating and enabling more stories like these? We are able to do what we do because of the generous support of an amazing group of people who give to Norwich Youth for Christ. You can give as a one-off or become part of our regular giving team. To find out more go to our website www.norwichyfc.co.uk